Virtual Caliphate

ISLAMIC EXTREMISTS AND THEIR WEBSITES

Virtual Caliphate
ISLAMIC EXTREMISTS AND THEIR WEBSITES

James Brandon

2008

CENTRE FOR SOCIAL COHESION

Centre for Social Cohesion
Clutha House
10 Storey's Gate
London SW1P 3AY
Tel: +44 (0)20 7222 8909
Fax: +44 (0)5 601527476
Email: mail@socialcohesion.co.uk
www.socialcohesion.co.uk

Director:
Douglas Murray

The Centre for Social Cohesion is a Civitas project

CIVITAS is a registered charity: No. 1085494.
Limited by guarantee.
Registered in England and Wales: No. 04023541

ISBN 978-1-903386-68-2

Printed in Great Britain by
The Cromwell Press
Trowbridge, Wiltshire

"The problem I find is that you start off listening to a speaker that you may not be familiar with, go though two or three lectures maybe. The next thing you find is they condemn the mujahideen here and there or start being apologetic about Terrorism in Islam. For me that's enough to switch off."[1]

Islambase administrator
19 April 2007

---

1 http://forum.islambase.co.uk/index.php?showtopic=181&mode=linearplus

Contents

The author

James Brandon is a senior research fellow at the Centre for Social Cohesion. He has an MA in Middle Eastern Studies from the School of Oriental and African Studies (SOAS). He has worked as a journalist for the BBC, Bloomberg and al-Jazeera, and has reported on Islamic issues from Europe, the Middle East and Africa. His previous reports for the CSC include *Hate on the state: How British libraries encourage Islamic extremism* and *Crimes of the Community: Honour-based violence in the UK*.

Acknowledgements

The author would like to thank Robin Simcox, Houriya Ahmed and Hannah Stuart of the Centre for Social Cohesion and Dominic Whiteman.

Introduction

There is a growing awareness that Islamic extremists around the world see the internet as an important tool for radicalising and recruiting new generations of terrorists. The British government has responded to this by criminalising 'the glorification of terror' in the 2006 Terrorism Act with specific reference to the distribution of pro-terrorist publications online. As this report shows, however, British extremists have now adapted to the government's measures and have found new ways to use the internet to spread hatred and promote violence.

■ *This report has found evidence that:*

❖ British extremists have set up several websites in order to distribute material justifying terrorist acts. Among these are texts and audio lectures by preachers imprisoned or deported for inciting violence and racial hatred.

❖ The same websites are being used to circulate texts and videos produced by members of al-Qaeda and other extremist Islamic groups. In addition, the websites distribute extreme Wahhabi and Salafi interpretations of Islam.

❖ The same websites are openly used by British extremists to organise public meetings and publicise their events. In addition, they use websites to distribute PDF leaflets and plan recruitment strategies.

❖ The websites also distribute messages from individuals imprisoned on terrorism-related offences.

Many of these activities are in clear breach of the 2006 Terrorism Act which criminalises the making of or circulation of any statement which "glorifies the commission or preparation (whether in the past, in the future or generally) of such acts or offences" of terrorism.[1]

The government appears to be either unaware of the material being

---

1 Terrorism Act 2006, (Chapter. 11) Part 1 — Offences (p. 2) http://www.opsi.gov.uk/acts/acts2006/pdf/ukpga_20060011_en.pdf

circulated on the internet or believes that it does not warrant prosecution. This report lays out the range of extremist material produced
and circulated by UK-based extremists online and shows how and why
the government's failure to prosecute those who run and contribute to
such websites puts the British public at risk of further terrorist attacks.

Methodology

This study is based on an online discussion on the password-protected forum of the islambase.co.uk website in which many of the website's most active users discussed their favourite Islamic websites. The discussion was initiated by one of the website's most active contributors, 'Hamza', and resulted in many of the most-active members of the forum listing 40 other sites. A full list of these websites and a copy of the discussion itself is available at the end of this report (see Appendices I and II).

This online discussion was significant because islambase.co.uk is widely acknowledged as the most significant website for UK-based Islamic extremists and hosts one of the largest English-language collections of jihadist texts and speeches available anywhere online. The website's discussion forums are widely used by former members of al-Muhajiroun and by followers of prominent preachers such as Abu Hamza, Sheikh Abdullah Faisal and Abu Izzadeen, who have all been convicted of inciting terrorism and soliciting murder in the UK. As this report shows, many Islambase users remain in direct contact with Bakri and Faisal by telephone, email and paltalk, an online chat programme and distribute messages from them through the Islambase website.

Because the report is focused on websites cited by Islambase users, it does not aim to provide a comprehensive account of all English-language websites run by or popular with Islamic radicals in the UK. Instead it aims to illustrate how extremists who were previously part of British groups such as al-Muhajiroun have re-organised themselves in response to British anti-terrorism measures by finding ways to continue their activities online. Out of the websites cited by Islambase users, the report concentrates on those sites are most active and which are both run by British-based Islamic extremists and focused primarily on the UK.

While the Islambase forum is password-protected, the website's sections on books, lectures and nasheeds are open to all. This report examines all both password-protected and un-protected parts of the site.

Glossary of Islamic terms

Aqeedah: creed

Bida: innovation

Dawa (Da'wa, Da'wah, Dawah): proselytising, invitation to Islam

Deen: literally "religion", often used to refer to Islam as a holistic way of living

Dunya: this world, earthly concerns (as opposed to the hereafter)

Fatwa: Islamic legal ruling

Fiqh: jurisprudence

Halal: permitted according to Islam

Haram: prohibited according to Islam

Insha'allah: if God wills

Jannah: paradise

Jihad: literally "struggle", usually defined in a religious sense as a "struggle in the path of Allah (God)" Interpretations range from a personal effort to live according to Islam, to defence and propagation of Islam by arms

Kaffir (Kafir) (pl. kuffar): someone who recognises the truth of Islam and then rejects it. However, it is often used as a culturally derogatory term to describe non-Muslims.

Kufr (n.): the rejection of truth

Nasheed: religiously themed song

Shaheed (shahid): literally means witness, but it is a term often used for martyrs.

Sharia: referred literally in the Quran as 'way'. As a term it refers to all Muslim religious codes and ethics as well as some laws. It is used as a synonym to fiqh.

Shirk: associating partners with Allah, i.e. idolatry

Subhana Wa Tala (SWT): the sacred and the mighty, a term normally used after saying Allah

Sul-allahu alayhi wasallam (SAW): peace be upon him, normally said in reference to the Prophet Mohammed

Sura: commonly used to mean a chapter in the Quran

Taghout: tyranny/oppressors

Takfir (takfeer): the practice of declaring an unbeliever

Ummah: Muslim community, the oneness of the community world-wide

CHAPTER 1:

Work by jailed, exiled or deported extremists

Islambase and other websites popular with Islambase users contain at least 100 recordings by four prominent preachers jailed by UK courts for inciting extremism and supporting terrorism. In addition, they contain numerous recordings by Omar Bakri, the former leader of al-Muhajiroun, who fled the UK shortly after the 7 July 2005 bombings. The websites are therefore the primary way for their British followers to access their teachings.

■ Abu Hamza al-Masri

Abu Hamza al-Masri (real name Mustafa Kamel Mustafa) is perhaps the most significant of the radical preachers active in the UK prior to the 7 July bombings. In the 1990s, Abu Hamza took control of the London's Finsbury Park Mosque turning it into a hub for jihadist movements and individuals as well as running a British radical group known as 'The supporters of Shariah'. In February 2006, Abu Hamza was found guilty of six counts of soliciting murder, three counts of using threatening, abusive or insulting words or behaviour and one count of possessing threatening, abusive or insulting recordings of sound.

Ken Macdonald QC, the director of public prosecutions said: "When we reviewed Abu Hamza's sermons, we were satisfied that he was directly and deliberately stirring up hatred against Jewish people and encouraging murder of those he referred to as non-believers. Not only did he repeatedly advocate that Muslims should kill non-believers, he set out to persuade his listeners that it was part of their religious duty to do so."[2]

Several prominent terrorists are believed to have been influenced by Abu Hamza's sermons. For example, Richard Reid, who attempted to bomb a trans-Atlantic airliner in December 2001, regularly attended

---

2 Crown Prosecution Service press release: 'Abu Hamza convicted of 11 charges'. 7 February 2006. http://www.cps.gov.uk/news/pressreleases/archive/2006/105_06.html

Abu Hamza's Finsbury Park mosque. Zacarias Moussaoui, the "twenti-eth hijacker" also attended the mosque as did Kamel Bourgass, an Alge-rian asylum seeker, who killed a police officer when his flat was raided in 2003 by police investigating a plot to manufacture ricin, a powerful poison.[3] In February 2008, Abu Hamza lost his final appeal against be-ing extradited to the US to stand trial on charges of attempting to set up a "terrorist training camp" in Oregon.[4]

The Islambase website contains recordings of 12 sermons by Abu Ham-za. Several of them denounce Jews and Christians and call for violence. These talks are similar to those which resulted in his convictions for incitement to murder and incitement to racial hatred. In one talk, enti-tled 'Bloody terrorism law', Abu Hamza blamed Jews for creating anti-terrorism laws:

> "[17:55][5] The children of Israel when they invent these laws, why did they invent these laws? – because they know that the promises of Allah, Subhana Wa Tala,[6] are true; they only want to delay so if it happens that it happens to their offsprings; because they know that Allah asked us to enjoin the good and forbid the evil."[7]

Other sections of the talk attacked the Jews as "the worst animals", cit-ing, as evidence, Sura al-Anfal, a chapter of the Quran:

> "[24:10] Allah described them [Jews] as "the worst of animals". The worst of animals! The worst of animals! Allah (swt) said the worst of animals are

---

3 *BBC:* 'Mosque's terror connections'. 8 February 2006. http://news.bbc.co.uk/1/hi/uk/4693804.stm

4 *BBC:* 'UK approves Abu Hamza extradition'. 7 February 2008. http://news.bbc.co.uk/1/hi/uk/7233671.stm

5 The numbers in square brackets refer to the time at which at the quotation begins.

6 *Subhana Wa Tala* (often abbreviated as SWT) is a phrase roughly translated as 'glori-fied and exulted' which Muslims traditionally say after mentioning Allah. Similar phrases are used by pious Muslims after referring Muhammad and in other instances. Such expressions re-occur very frequently in talks available on Islambase-related web-sites. For ease of reading, they have been removed from the transcriptions used in this report. They have however been retained when they are appear in online discussions on forums.

7 http://islambase.co.uk/index.php?option=com_content&task=view&id=445&Itemid=181

2

the kuffar [non-Muslims] – it is in Sura al-Anfal. The worst of animals are the kuffar and Allah said because they go back on their covenant and they don't fulfil their pledges. Any time you do a pledge they go backwards. Allah told us already – if you do a pledge, if you do a covenant, do peace treaty with you, the result is that they will have to break it – especially Jews."

He also said that the Jews and Christians should be fought until they accepted living under Muslim rule and paid the *jizya*, a discriminatory tax on non-Muslims:

"[24:49] Allah said this is your aim, it is to fight them until they pay the tax, the jizya, for Muslims in humiliation. So that should be done until you do that. What if you should no do it? – You should take the means to do it. You should go if you cannot do it, our children [can do it]; we should prepare, we should pave the roads for our children to do it."

In another talk, '[The] West against all religions', which apparently dates to early 2002, Abu Hamza told audience that Islam and the West were incompatible:[8]

"[19:13] The worst is these kind of people who separated the soul from the body and they are killing the soul and feeding the body at the expense of the soul and the spiritual matter; this is the West and by definition it's compatible not [sic] only with Islam; it's not compatible with God the creator; it's not compatible with Christianity; it's not compatible with Judaism. So they want us to dilute Islam to give a version of Islam so we can go to the mosque in the morning and go to the pub with them in the evening and we share wives in the afternoon."

In another talk 'Voting is kufr and haram', Abu Hamza described democracy as un-Islamic because it allows mankind to make laws which are not based on the Quran. He adds that sexual and religious equality are also incompatible with Islam:

"[22:50] Democracy is shirk [idolatry]. [There is] Shirk in legislation. Shirk in lies. Shirk in everything. And also it's bida [an innovation] to do it. Why it is bida? One man, one vote. What do you mean 'one man, one vote?' One man, one vote. One sahabi [companion of Muhammad], one vote; one prostitute, one vote. One Muslim, one vote; one kafir, one vote."

---

8 http://islambase.co.uk/index.php?option=com_content&task=view&id=456&Itemid=181

He further said that it is against Islam for Muslims to be treated equally with non-Muslims:

> "[24:22] But do you want to make Abu Bakr Sadiq or one of the prophets like a prostitute or a whore or a kaffir women who doesn't care about anything, except earning from haram and doing obscenity. Is that a principle of Islam? Isn't that a bida in Islam? So, you see now, it's [democracy's] reality is kufr [disbelief]; it's methodology is bida. What are Muslim to do with these kind of things, except to fight them?"

The salafiyyah-jadeedah.tripod.com website contains an online copy of 'Ruling By Man-made Law – Is It Minor or Major Kufr? Explaining the Words of Ibn Abbas' by Abu Hamza'. The book, written in 1996, is a lengthy attack on secularism and on governments which rule by anything but the Sharia.[9] The same website also contains an 18-page response written by Abu Hamza to critics of the book.[10]

The Islambase website contains a PDF of another book by Abu Hamza, 'The Khawaarij and Jihaad' written in 2000. Khawaarij refers to a group of 7th century Muslim heretics and the book mainly deals with issues relating to jihadist operations in Algeria. On 17 November 2007, 'Hamza', one of the most active members of the Islambase forum, recommended the book to another reader who was seeking information "on the beliefs of the khawaarij", saying:

> "May Allah(swt) reward Abu Maryam [another name for Abu Hamza]. We miss him dearly."[11]

Islambase users often refer respectfully to Abu Hamza's teachings and many cite him as one of their favourite speakers.[12] Many also closely follow his ongoing legal battles. On 7 February, 'Abu Abdur Rahman' responded to news that Abu Hamza had lost his appeal against deportation to the US by writing:

> "It just made me feel sick, the feeling where your tongue becomes heavy and your heart feels empty. Only by Allah's will, is there any hope for him other-

---

9 http://salafiyyah-jadeedah.tripod.com/Legislation/Ruling_by_man_made_law.html

10 http://salafiyyah-jadeedah.tripod.com/Legislation/refutation_of_allegations.doc

11 http://forum.islambase.co.uk/index.php?showtopic=1790

12 http://forum.islambase.co.uk/index.php?showtopic=181&mode=linearplus]

wise everyone knows what sort of future he is looking at. May Allah swt send his wrath upon the mujrimeen [those who do not follow Islam] and destroy their nations by the hand of truth and deliver to them storms and hurricanes, calamity after calamity and tragedy followed by despair and grief. May Allah swt protect our dear brother and make for him jannah [paradise] his final abode. Allahu mustaan."[13]

On other occasions, Islambase members use the website to request recordings of particular lectures given ny Abu Hamza. In July 2007, for example, 'Slave Of AllaaH', a female Islambase members requested three Ramadan sermons by Abu Hamza(including one titled 'Ramadan in Chechnya').[14] After some discussion other readers were able to provide her with all three recordings.

■ Sheikh Abdullah Faisal

During the late 1990s and early 2005, Sheikh Abdullah al-Faisal, a Jamaican-born convert to Islam, was one of the most significant extremist preachers active in the UK. Faisal's nationwide lectures are believed to have played an important role in persuading several British Muslims that it was an Islamic obligation to carry out jihadist attacks. Three lectures given by Faisal in Beeston, near Leeds, apparently played a key role in radicalising the 7 July 2005 bombers and Muhammad Sidique Khan, the group's leader, is said to have possessed several of his tapes.[15] Faisal is also reported to have influenced Germaine Lindsay, a black convert to Islam who also became one of the 7 July bombers.[16] In March 2003, al-Faisal was found guilty of two counts of soliciting murder, two counts of using threatening words and behaviour and one count of "distributing threatening abusive or insulting recordings of sound".[17]

---

13 http://forum.islambase.co.uk/index.php?showtopic=2419

14 http://forum.islambase.co.uk/index.php?showtopic=1527&hl=Abu+Hamza]

15 *The Sunday Times:* 'British imam praises London tube bombers'. 12 February 2006. http://www.timesonline.co.uk/tol/news/uk/article730019.ece

16 *BBC:* Race hate cleric Faisal deported (25 May 2007) http://news.bbc.co.uk/1/hi/uk/6691701.stm

17 Crown Prosecution Service: Violent extremism and related criminal offences http://www.cps.gov.uk/Publications/prosecution/violent_extremism.html

He received a nine-year prison sentence.[18] In May 2007, he was released and deported to Jamaica. [19]

The Islambase website contains audio recordings of several of al-Faisal's sermons given prior to his imprisonment. One recording, 'Tafsir Surah Al Kafirounon', discussing the Quranic chapter 'Al-Kafiroun', contains denunciations of democracy as *shirk* (idolatry) and of non-Muslims in general. In this talk, he accused the British government of using "germ warfare" to spread "corruption" among Muslim communities in the UK:

> "Germ warfare. They allow prostitutes to operate freely in areas that are predominantly Muslim areas. Drugs warfare. They allow drugs pushers to see their dope in predominantly Muslims areas – you walks around like a zombie. "[20]

In another talk 'Challenges facing the Muslim youth' on the Islambase site, Faisal compared the UK to a "cancer" which is corrupting young Muslims:

> "[0:28] You can't live in a cancer without becoming affected by that cancer."[21]

He then tells his audience that western society is little more than a plot to corrupt Muslims:

> "[16:40] When you were in school, they taught you to sing. All of you used to sing this, you can't deny it. You are guilty of singing this song 'hey diddle diddle, the cat and the fiddle, the cow jumped over the moon'. All of you used to sing that song. Now this song is not innocent. You think it's innocent fun. But it's not innocent. You know why? It's impossible for a cow to jump over the moon. But why do they teach you this? To make lies … To make lies become the normal in your psyche, in your mentality from a very tender age. Also they taught you the story of Snow White and the Seven Dwarves. Now what

---

18 *BBC:* 'Hate preaching cleric jailed'. 7 March 2003. http://news.bbc.co.uk/1/hi/england/2829059.stm

19 B*BC:* 'Race hate cleric Faisal deported'. 25 May 2007. http://news.bbc.co.uk/1/hi/uk/6691701.stm

20 http://islambase.co.uk/index.php?option=com_content&task=view&id=625&Itemid=181

21 http://islambase.co.uk/index.php?option=com_content&task=view&id=556&Itemid=181

is the purpose behind this story? This story was to preach white supremacy. They have seven midgets looking on this beautiful woman lying on the bed, this white woman, seven midgets looking at her and they're crying and they were fearing for her life. It is also to promote female promiscuity, that 'look, this woman, she has seven midgets underneath her charm. She's so pretty, she has seven men going crazy over her'. So the average woman in this society, I wouldn't be surprised if she'd like to have seven men underneath her charms, because she was classically conditioned by this story towards white supremacy and to practice female promiscuity."

The talk contains additional attacks on "free-mixing" between men and women, perfume, democracy, music and inter-faith initiatives. He also outlines the punishments that would be carried out in an "Islamic state":

"[7:20] The punishment for those who wage war against Allah and his messenger, and strive with might and means to spread mischief in the land is that they should be killed and crucified, or their hands and feet should be cut off from opposite sides, or they should be banished from the land…so we kill drug smugglers, people who smuggle cannabis and heroin and cocaine in the Islamic state."

In 'Islam Under Siege', a talk which apparently dates to shortly before the Taliban were toppled in 2001, Faisal argues that Islam is in an eternal and inevitable conflict against non-Muslim cultures and peoples:

"[0:49] The unbelievers … are enemies of Allah and his messenger, and are enemies of the Muslims. Allah tells us the struggle between Islam and the kufr, between Muslims and the kaffirs, the unbelievers, is a never ending struggle…The Christians and the Jews will never be contented with you until you follow their evil and corrupted evil way of life."[22]

He adds that the "aim and objective of non-Muslims'" "is to spread their filth throughout the entire universe" and says that conflict between Muslims and non-Muslims is "never-ending" – for which he blames the Jews:

"[24:38] The battle between truth and falsehood is never-ending…now you are in conflict; your way of life, al-Islam, is in conflict with the way of life of the people who are ruling the world. So who are ruling the world? The people

---

22 http://islambase.co.uk/index.php?option=com_content&task=view&id=356&Itemid=181

who are ruling the world unfortunately happen to be the Jews, who are the henchman of the dajal [anti-Christ]."

The talk reaches its climax with a call for jihad:

"[1:15:17] there's only one way forward for you now, and that is jihad…and even if you don't want jihad, the kaffirs are going to bring it to your doorstep. Because a Muslim woman walking down the road, like what happened in Swindon, and they beat her with baseball bat…they are killing you in Chechnya, killing you in Palestine, killing you in Iraq, every day, 24 hours a day, every day. So the days of soft Islam are over. Because the kaffirs, even if you don't want to wake up, they are making sure you wake up by killing your men, putting your scholars in prison, raping your woman, robbing you of your natural resources…occupying your holy lands, robbing you of your natural resources, putting your men in concentration camps, putting your women in rape camps, killing your scholars."

An additional 30 lectures by Faisal are available on the kalamullah. com website, some of which apparently date as far back as 1997.[23] The Islambase website, however, also contains a recent interview given by Faisal in December 2007 to Jamaican TV in which he renounced many of his former extremist beliefs.[24] However, the site also contains an interview given on 10 February 2008 to a US Muslim website, in which he says:

[02:45] "The infidels would like to carry out ethnic cleansing against the Muslims in order to usurp our natural resources – that is on their agenda. So any cleric or any sheikh who preaches self-defence they say 'well that self-defence which you are preaching or jihad is actually murder; you would like to murder us'."[25]

On the Islambase forum, readers frequently discuss al-Faisal and ask for his talks to be put online. On 3 July 2007, "Abdulrahmanal-Muhajir" wrote:

"Can someone please upload as many audio talks of Shaykh Abdullah Faisal

---

23 http://www.kalamullah.com/faisal.html

24 http://islambase.co.uk/index.php?option=com_content&task=view&id=1034&Itemid=181

25 http://islambase.co.uk/index.php?option=com_content&task=view&id=1095&Itemid=181

(May allah look after him). I know there are a few sites that have his talks but they are very selective."[26]

On 9 March 2008, 'abu aisha' posted a request for al-Faisal's lecture, "Devil's Deception of the Murji'ah" about the Shia to be made available online.[27] Similarly, on 12 January 2008, 'moderate_muslim' posted a request for someone to post al-Faisal's lecture '21st Century House niggers'[28] in which he attacked Muslims who co-operated with the British government. This request provoked an online discussion of al-Faisal's teachings, with one reader, 'Tarbiya', questioning al-Faisal's use of takfir, the salafi practice of declaring other Muslims to be kuffar:

"Brother Faisal has mistakes in his 'usool of Takfeer."

This provoked another reader, 'Ibrahim atturki' (Ibrahim the Turk) to defend Faisal, writing:

"Can you please if possible quote which lecture and which statement you are talking about as im not aware of such mistakes."

'Tarbiya' then offers to make a phone call to al-Faisal in Jamaica to clarify his present position on the use of takfir, writing:

"I have his number in Jamaica and will, bi'ithnillah, be speaking to him and getting his permission to record a short Q&A with him very soon."

Other readers also offer apparently first-hand recollections of al-Faisal and Abu Hamza. 'Abu Hamza al-Britani' writes:

"I have not heard SF [Sheikh Faisal] make chain takfir – ie. If you don't believe he is kafir then you are kafir".

'Islam Roast' adds that:

"These issues of the takfeer were resolved years ago between brother faisal

26 [http://forum.islambase.co.uk/index.php?showtopic=751]

27 http://forum.islambase.co.uk/index.php?showtopic=2786

28 http://forum.islambase.co.uk/index.php?showtopic=2168&st=0

and abu hamza ... there was closed door meetings between sheikh faisal and sheikh abu hamza".

This exchange shows that many Islambase users are themselves veterans of the late 1990s/early-2000s jihadist networks and still have close links to radical preachers like Faisal. In addition, there is evidence of Islambase users treating Faisal as a general spiritual advisor. For instance, on 2 April 2008, 'Umm Sabah' wrote that she had questioned Faisal online about the correct Islamic way to bring up adopted children.[29]

■ Omar Bakri

Along with Abu Hamza and Abdullah Faisal, Omar Bakri was one of the most high-profile radical preachers active in the UK prior to the 7 July bombings. After coming to the UK in 1986, he helped establish the British branch of Hizb ut-Tahrir, a global organisation aiming to re-establish the Caliphate, before setting up al-Muhajiroun, one of the most extreme Islamic groups in the UK which was disbanded in October 2004.[30] Shortly after the 7 July bombings, Bakri moved to Lebanon where he presently lives. He has not been charged with any crimes in the UK. Since moving to Lebanon, he has continued to communicate with his followers through the internet, principally using paltalk, an internet chat service offering cheap, online telephone and video communication, to give lectures on politics and Islam.

The Islambase website hosts 48 different talks by Bakri.[31] Some of his talks date to before his 2005 move to Lebanon; others are more recent. Many of his lectures denounce non-Muslims for spreading 'corruption' and call for attacks on Muslims who do not support Bakri's vision of Islam and endorse jihadist attacks around the world. In one talk 'The Jews and the Christians', Bakri said:

> "[44:44 – 45:12] Those Kuffar they are teething [stealing], polluting the Muslim mind in the name of interfaith, in the name of integration, in the name of 'if you're not going to love us we are going to call you terrorists', they are really

---

29 http://forum.islambase.co.uk/index.php?showtopic=3205&hl=milk]

30 *BBC:* 'New group replaces al-Muhajiroun' (18 November 2005) http://news.bbc.co.uk/1/hi/uk/4449714.stm

31 http://islambase.co.uk/index.php?option=com_content&task=category&sectionid=3 3&id=75&Itemid=181

blackmailing everybody, their whole deen is false, they don't believe it's false, their own life is completely false."[32]

In another recorded talk, 'Mischief Makers in the UK', apparently dating to early 2007, Bakri denounces secularism as a corruption and a form of kufr:

"[07:37 – 08:39] You Muslims today if you want to believe in deen [Islamic religion], you don't want to establish it in power and to make it a superior and nothing superseded, you're going to become like the Christian, you're going to said: 'oh mighty Allah mind your business in the Mosque and we mind our life ourselves in the society and in the parliament'. That's exactly what secularism is about. It's a form of Kufr in high level of corruption. It is a form of shirk in high level of directing or diverting all mighty Allah attribute to somebody and people are accepting that. They deserve to be humiliated. They deserve to be down because they accept it to be slave of man instead of slave of all mighty Allah. They accept it to be slave of the benefit and interest and all mighty dollars than to be the servant of all mighty Allah the creator the only creator, the only provider the only commander."[33]

In another speech, 'The Legacy of Amir Khattab', Bakri discussed the life of Ibn Khattab, the former leader of foreign jihadists in Chechnya, saying the Chechens' actions are a sign that "[15:41] when the jihad fever spreads, no-one can stop it; it will go from mountain to mountain, from city to city." Bakri compares attacks carried out by jihadists in Chechnya and on 11 September to those carried out by Muhammad and his followers:

"[13:50] September 11; those beautiful mujahideen, they remind us about old days; how Muslims used to be devoted and fight in the sake of Allah and how they sacrificed everything."[34]

Citing the attack by Chechen mujahideen on the Moscow theatre in October 2002, he said that women should play a key role in future jihadist operations:

---

32 http://islambase.co.uk/index.php?option=com_content&task=view&id=738&Itemid=181

33 http://islambase.co.uk/index.php?option=com_content&task=view&id=583&Itemid=181

34 http://islambase.co.uk/index.php?option=com_content&task=view&id=400&Itemid=181

"[14:51] The Muslim sister give us the example that the woman in Islam is not only mother, is not only sister, is not only daughter, is not only honour … in the time of crisis, she is a Muslim and is a shield for the Muslim Ummah and she is a fighter to fight to the sake of Allah [swt]."

The salafiyyah-jadeedah.tripod.com website contains a copy of Omar Bakri's short article '6 Reasons why all the rulers are Murtad'. This article was taken originally from al-Muhajiroun's now defunct website (muhajiroun.com).[35] The article stresses the importance of pronouncing takfir against other Muslims; i.e. declaring them to have rejected Islam and thus to be liable to be killed:

"We worship Allah (subhana wa Ta'ala) by making takfeer – declaring a person to be Kafir. At-Takfeer is an obligation upon all Muslims. Those who do not make takfeer are Mushriks [polytheists] as the first pillar of Tawheed [Islamic monotheism] requires one to make takfeer by declaring those who Allah calls Kafir to be Kafir."

On Islambase forums, Omar Bakri is frequently mentioned by readers but rarely with unquestioning reverence. For example, on 17 March 2008, a discussion about people leaving al-Muhajiroun quickly turned into a discussion of the shortcomings of Omar Bakri, the group's leader.[36] 'Abu Hamza al-Britani' writes:

"OBM [Omar Bakri Mohammad] made mistakes. Fact. It's not because of any hatred towards the man but simply because it needs to be hammered home that no man (except Mustafa [Muhammad] (pbuh)) is allowed to be blind followed – OBM is not infallible."

He also recalls that many al-Muhajiroun members had been afraid to criticise Bakri:

"And while we were in the jama' [mosque/study circle] we did not correct shiekh or question him if we felt something was not right or needed clarification. Not only on the fiqh [jurisprudence] issues but even in the English language!! It was a trait of ours to follow him to the extent that if he made an error in the English language or used a word in the wrong context we would adopt it rather than correct him."

---

35 http://salafiyyah-jadeedah.tripod.com/Governments/Reasons_Murtad.htm

36 http://forum.islambase.co.uk/index.php?showtopic=2898&hl

But while many Islambase users express doubts about Bakri's ideas and scholarship, they continue to ask his advice – perhaps simply because he is easier to contact than others such as Abu Hamza or Abu Qatada now in prison. For example, on 3 July 2007, 'Abu Shiblain' contacts Bakri to ask if it is permissible for Muslim to debate at Speaker's Corner in London. Bakri replied that it was permissible but that there were "better places".[37]

■ Abu Qatada al-Filistini

Before his arrest in London in October 2002, Abu Qatada al-Filistani, a Jordanian salafist preacher, was the most prominent jihadist scholar in the UK. Abu Qatada (also known as Omar Mahmoud Mohammed Othman) was widely seen as having more theological authority than better-known individuals like Abu Hamza or Omar Bakri and issued fatwas on behalf of the GIA (*Groupe Islamique Armé*) in Algeria. In the late 1990s and early 2000s, Abu Qatada was in direct contact with numerous members and supporters of al-Qaeda. For instance, when he was arrested in February 2001, police discovered £170,000 in cash in his home, including £805 in an envelope labelled "For the Mujahedin in Chechnya".[38] He has also allegedly played a key role in radicalising several key al-Qaeda individuals[39]. Most notably, 18 video recordings of Abu Qatada's talks were discovered in the Hamburg flats of Muhammad Atta, the leader of the 11 September attacks.[40] In February 2007, the Special Immigration Appeals Commission ruled that "He has given advice to many terrorist groups and individuals, whether formerly a spiritual adviser to them or not. His reach and the depth of his influence in that respect is formidable, even incalculable. "[41] He is currently in Belmarsh prison, appealing against extradition to Jordan.

----

37 http://forum.islambase.co.uk/index.php?showtopic=734&mode=linear

38 *BBC:* 'Profile: Abu Qatada'. 27 February 2007. http://news.bbc.co.uk/1/hi/uk/4141594.stm

39 *The Daily Telegraph:* 'Extremist who came to UK on fake passport'. 27 February 2007. http://www.telegraph.co.uk/news/main.jhtml?xml=/news/2007/02/26/nqatada226.xml

40 *BBC:* 'Profile: Abu Qatada'. 27 February 2007. http://news.bbc.co.uk/1/hi/uk/4141594.stm, The Guardian: 'Guantanamo UK'. 14 December 2003. http://www.guardian.co.uk/world/2003/dec/14/humanrights.usa

41 *BBC:* 'Cleric loses deportation appeal'. 26 February 2007. http://news.bbc.co.uk/1/hi/uk/6396447.stm

The Islambase website contains 17 audio recordings by Abu Qatada. The recordings, however, are all in Arabic which limits their audience in British radical circles. In addition, Islambase users regularly distribute links to recorded talks by Abu Qatada which are stored on other websites. For example, on 29 March 2008, 'Abu Dujanah' posted links on the Islambase forum to an additional 25 video recordings which are stored on another website, archive.org.[42]

In talk available on the Islambase website, 'Wajib al Muslim' (The duty of Muslims), Abu Qatada, speaking in Arabic, says that it is the duty of Muslim to wage jihad against "oppressors" (both Muslim and non-Muslim) who do not fully apply sharia law until the caliphate has been re-established:

"[14:21] The only way to have a khilafa is through jihad."

He also explicitly tells his audience that it is the duty of Muslims in the Arab world to physically attack and kill secularists, whom he describes as "kaffirs":

"[17:51] Our countries have been infiltrated by kaffirs. It is a farid [duty] for us to turn our swords on to them and kill them."

In another recorded speech entitled 'Seerah' (The Path) available on Islambase, Abu Qatada slanders Jews and encourages Muslims to fight them:

"[21:56] In Jewish law, when a Jew enters a village in war or peace it is his duty to rape the land, take kill [sic] the men and turn the women into slaves. He will take the land and the money and that is what that religion says. This war is for existence, to exist or not exist. You see the West supports that state [Israel], they are on their side. The west says it is an economic relationship but it is not. "

He then warns his listeners about a final battle between Muslims and pagans which will "rid the planet of the Jews":

"[23:48] There will be a great battle against the 'wathaniyah' [pagans/Jews and Christians] where the saviour will come back to this earth, the king with an army in the sky, killing the Jews, to wipe them out and rid of the planet of the Jews."

42 http://forum.islambase.co.uk/index.php?showtopic=3134&hl=Abu+Hamza]

14

He also says that a true Muslim should seek and desire martyrdom:

"[40:41] Jews hate death. A Muslim seeks death and longs for it the only way to achieve our goals is through Jihad. We must fight the kafirs. We can't reason with them. We can't reach a compromise and we can't be friends."

In another Arabic lecture, entitled 'Tark Shahwaat' [the path of desire], Abu Qatada tells his audience that a "love of life" is corrupting Muslims and dividing them:

"[three to four minutes into the talk] The dunya [love of life] is what is sepa-rating Muslims. For it they are fighting us and because of her it is dividing and spreading immoral behaviour."

The sawtulislam website contains an article written by Abu Qatada about his imprisonment. The article, apparently written within the last few years and posted on the website on 16 December 2007, says:

"Prison is a trial; it will either break [you], or squeeze [you], or profit [you] so that the imprisoned one will emerge purified of all impurities – impurities of thought and impurities within his Nafs [soul], so that his insight ascends, and his Nafs is polished in its development and training."[43]

Many Islambase users rate Abu Qatada above better known figures like Omar Bakri and Abu Hamza. On 22 March 2008, 'Abu Abdur-Rahman' wrote on a discussion:

"[Abu Qatada] must be the most well known of all the people in the UK when it comes to knowledge. This man has tazkiyah [lit. meaning, purification of the soul] from all over the world and is held in very high esteem. This man even received an endorsement from Dr Ayman [Zawahiri]."[44]

He added that

"Never in my life did I think the day would come that I would have a conver-sation with a people that claim to love Jihad and [at the same time] question

---

43 http://www.sawtulislam.com/?cat=45. In mid-April, as this report was being pre-pared for publication, the format of the sawtulislam website was changed and a large amount of texts and audio material was put in a password-protected section of the site.

44 http://forum.islambase.co.uk/index.php?showtopic=2898&hl=tazkiyah&st=120

15

Sheik Abu Qatada. It's so comical that I wouldn't even know where to begin to defend this stupidity"[45]

On other occasions, Islambase users have shared links to additional Abu Qatada lectures. For instance, on 22 May 2007, the Islambase administrator posted links to an additional 96 Abu Qatada lectures stored on the archive.org website.[46]

On 8 May, Islambase users responded with delight to news that Abu Qatada had been granted bail. A typical response came from Hamza who wrote:

"Allah ho Akbar!! [God is Great]. Allah ho Akbar!! Allah ho Akbar!!"[47]

■ Abu Izzadeen

Abu Izzadeen, a convert to Islam also known as Omar Brookes, is a former member of al-Muhajiroun. In September 2006, he famously heckled John Reid, the then Home Secretary, at a meeting in East London, accusing him of coming to a "Muslim area" in which the government had no authority. [48] In April 2008 he was found guilty of inciting terrorism and raising funds for terrorism.[49] He was sentenced to four and a half years imprisonment.[50]

The sawtuislam website contains several recordings of Abu Izzadeen's talks. In one lecture, 'The Integration Plot', Abu Izzadeen criticised both

---

45 http://forum.islambase.co.uk/index.php?showtopic=2898&st=120

46 http://forum.islambase.co.uk/index.php?showtopic=294&hl=qatada]

47 [http://forum.islambase.co.uk/index.php?showtopic=3714]

48 *BBC:* 'Reid heckled during Muslim speech'. 20 September 2006. http://news.bbc. co.uk/1/hi/uk/5362052.stm, *The Guardian:* 'Reid barracked during speech to Muslim parents'. 20 September 2006. http://www.guardian.co.uk/world/2006/sep/20/terrorism. immigrationpolicy

49 *BBC:* "Arrogant' Muslim preacher jailed' (18 April 2008) http://news.bbc.co.uk/1/hi/ uk/7354397.stm

50 *The Daily Telegraph:* 'Muslim preacher Abu Izzadeen jailed for four and a half years' (21 April 2008) http://www.telegraph.co.uk/news/main.jhtml?xml=/news/2008/04/18/ nizzadeen218.xml

mainstream Muslim organisations and the UK government for encouraging Muslims to consider themselves British:

> "[11:30] What is my identity? Am I a British Muslim? No, brothers: A British Muslims is the one that's his allegiance is to the queen; his allegiance is to a red book – the passport ; his allegiance is to the JSA [Job Seeker's Allowance] and the income support. No brothers – that's not the Muslim. The Muslim – his allegiance is to Allah and the nebi [prophet] and to the Muslims."[51]

In another talk on sawtulislam, 'Da'wah in the UK', Abu Izzadeen cited Ibn Qudamah al-Maqdisi (d. 1224 AD), a medieval Hanbali scholar, to argue that Muslims in the UK should not perform hijrah (emigrate) but instead that they have an obligation to live in non-Muslim states – traditionally known as the dar al-harb (land of war) – in order to convert non-Muslims to Islam:

> "[54:50] Ibn Qudamah al-Mugdisi in his *Kitab al-Mughni*, he said: for the one who lives in dar al-harb [non-Muslim countries] and he gives dawa, calls for Islam, and around him is what? Islam everywhere! he covers himself in Islam. Where he lives becomes a spot of Islam so that for him to leave, to make hijrah, is haram, it is a fard [obligation] for him to stay. Your presence in the UK – never underestimate it, my dear Muslim brothers."

He also said that dawa and jihad are complementary as they both aim to make Islam dominant in the world and adds that as a result Muslims should not "neglect either one of them":

> "[01:14:51]The dawa and the jihad go side-by-side; they never leave each other. So never neglect each one of them."

Abu Izzadeen seems popular with the users of Islambase and other radical Islamic websites. On 27 January 2008, one of Abu Izzadeen's talks, entitled 'Ahlus Sunnah wal Jama'ah Explained' and which promotes traditionalist Wahabi teachings, was uploaded onto the sawtulislam website. In it, Abu Izzadeen discussed how to practice Islam according to salafi interpretations. The same day as the lecture was put online on sawtulislam.com, 'Abdul-Aziz' praised the talk, writing:

> "Mashallah!, may allah swt make us all followers of ahlus sunnah wal jammah! and may allah keep Abu Izzadeen in good health, and firm in the deen and i pray that allah swt releases him from captivity of the kuffar! may allah release all the brothers who are behind bars. i pray that all the brothers who have

---

51 http://www.sawtulislam.com/?p=123

their trials which have started, that their cases get thrown out. oh allah please release them! oh allah please release them! oh allah please release them! Ameen! Ameen! Ameen!"[52]

It seems likely that Abu Izzadeen's popularity has been boosted by his trial which Islambase users see as evidence of his commitment and sincerity. On 5 April 2008, for example, 'Hamza' wrote that "he was one of the very few genuine people that put thier money where thier [sic] mouth was."[53]

---

52 http://www.sawtulislam.com/?p=175

53 http://forum.islambase.co.uk/index.php?showtopic=2898&st=340

CHAPTER 2:

Material by other
UK-based extremists

UK-based websites popular with Islambase users also host numerous audio-files of speeches and talks given by extremist preachers who are still active in the UK and who have not been convicted for terrorism-related offences. Unlike the recordings by better known pro-jihadist clerics, which are often recorded abroad or which date to prior to their imprisonment, these other recordings are often posted online just days after being made and are often recordings of talks and lectures given to audiences at events in London or Luton.

■ *Anjem Choudary*

Anjem Choudary was formerly the deputy-leader of al-Muhajiroun, the organisation run by Omar Bakri. Since the dissolution of al-Muhajiroun and the departure of Bakri to Lebanon, Choudary has assumed a leadership role over some former members of this and other groups. A trained lawyer, he is adept at avoiding falling foul of laws prohibiting incitement to violence. Many of his talks call on his listeners to work to raise awareness of Muslims imprisoned under anti-terrorism laws.

In a talk entitled 'Our Duty to the Aseer' (hostages) available on sawtu-lislam, Choudary called on listeners to support and remember Muslims held prisoner by "the kuffar":

> [1:01:40] "You need to do something; raise awareness; make the Muslims aware about the Muslims in captivity, create public awareness, raise the funds to release them to give their bail. If you can release them in other ways, re-lease them."[54]

Choudary's talk contains frequent attempts to highlight perceived in-equalities between Muslims and non-Muslims in the UK, on several oc-

---

54 http://www.sawtulislam.com/?p=161

casions referring to his followers who were imprisoned following their role in demonstrations against the Danish cartoons:[55]

[1:10:40] "Remember the paedophile. What was his name? Mr Peter File. [laughter from audience] Mr Peter File abused 25 children. The youngest one was 18 months old – he got nothing at all. When there was public outrage, they gave him an 18-month suspended sentence. Abdul Muhid, on the other hand, held up a nasty placard and got six years. Six years! That's what they think of a nasty placard. In fact it was a very nice placard – but they got six years for holding up a placard."

He also described how Muslims around the world were being oppressed and had no means to fight back, drawing comparisons between the condition of British Muslims and their counter-parts worldwide:

[01:10] "There's no doubt that the Kuffar have the upper hand over the Muslims. We can see that by the Kufr law. No country in the world today has Islamic law and order. The whole world is dar al-Kufr or dar al-harb whether you talk about Sudan or Afghanistan or Somalia or Iraq. No-one has declared Imar al-Emara, general authority for the Muslims worldwide. Some pockets of Imar al-Khasa, specific authority for the Muslims – yes, in some areas but today we do not have a shield behind which we can defend ourselves, behind which we can fight, behind which we can launch the armies of jihad to liberate our Muslim brothers and sisters and even to liberate the land and remove the obstacles in the way of implementing the sharia."

This talk received positive reviews from several sawtulislam users. One reader, 'Saiful Islam' ('Sword of Islam') wrote, "May Allah preserve Sheikh Anjem! Ameen!". Others began discussing whether Choudary was a Sheikh, a Dai'ee (one who calls people to Islam) or a mujtahid (interpreter of the Quran). Dismissing these discussions, 'Izzah' wrote:

"The same could be asked about the likes of Abdullah el-Faisal, Abu Hamza, Anwar al-Awlaki, etc. But is it relevant? What matters is that they are daaies that speak the haq [truth]."

In another talk on sawtulislam, Choudary discusses the practice of takfir which he describes as "taking someone outside or out of the camp of Islam and putting them in the camp of Kufr" [00:25]:

---

55 BBC: 'Four men jailed over cartoon demo'. 18 July 2007. http://news.bbc.co.uk/1/hi/uk/6904622.stm

"[00:32] This is a very dangerous topic because if we take someone outside the camp of Islam then they no longer have sanctity for their life or their wealth and plus their children are no longer attributed to them and they don't inherit and their wife is no longer halal for them and plus we have bara' [hatred] for them as well – we make distance from them. Our relationship with them is one of asking them to repent."[56]

Elsewhere he cited Muhammad ibn Abdul-Wahhab, the founder of Wahhabism, and gave historical examples of Muslims – and Muhammad himself – denouncing people as kuffar and then killing them:

"[1:43:26] We have many examples of how individuals were killed because they apostatised. Those people who say you cannot declare takfir against an individual are wrong because we have examples from the time of the Sahaba [the companions of Muhammad] and the prophet himself."

The sawtulislam website regularly features press statements issued by Choudary. For example, on 23 March 2008, the website posted a statement from Choudary in response to claims made in the *News of the World* that he was recruiting British Muslims for jihad.[57] Choudary denied the claims, writing:

"I would like to re-iterate once again that I firmly believe that Muslims in Britain live here under a covenant of security, where in return for their lives and wealth being secure they are not allowed to target the life or wealth of anyone, Muslim or non-Muslim, government or otherwise. Muslims in Britain are engaged in a political and ideological struggle in the UK and not a military one, as opposed to what the News of the World would have everyone believe!"

One reader calling himself 'Muslim', responded to the News of the World's allegations saying, "Bunch of liars. Would you expect less from them when their government goes to war based on lies."[58]

Discussions on the Islambase forum and other website frequently refer to Choudary with affection although he is rarely viewed as a scholar or a cleric even by his most ardent supporters. For example, on 22 March, forum members discussed whether Choudary could be called a 'Sheikh'

---

56 http://www.sawtulislam.com/?p=276

57 http://www.sawtulislam.com/?cat=53

58 http://www.sawtulislam.com/?cat=53

as he lacked the necessary scholarly credentials. Nonetheless, many Is-lambase readers say that they are inspired by his talks.[59] On 1 January 2008, a woman, "Umm Abdullah", nominated him as one of her favourite speakers:

> "Bro Anjem, Ive not heard many of his talks but the ones that I have heard of him I have found my self able to concentrate. Im not one of these people that can concentrate for a long time, but the bro has a good fast and fluent flow to his talks. Im excited because hes gonna be doing study circles in Leicester from next week inshallah."[60]

■ Abu Bashir al-Tartusi

The Islambase website features recordings of 14 lectures delivered by Abu Basir al-Tartusi, a Syrian salafi cleric based in London.[61] Al-Tartusi (his real name is Abd-al Mun'em Mustafa Halima) has been described as one of "the primary Salafi opinion-makers guiding the jihadi movement" through his role in providing theological justification for a wide variety of jihadist operations[62]. After the 7 July bombings, however, he began to retract some of his earlier statements, voicing criticism of the bombers' decisions to carry out attacks against civilian targets within the UK.[63]

Tartusi's most significant lecture on Islambase is 'The Covenant of Security in Islam' in which he argues that British Muslims are forbidden from carrying out jihad within the UK. In the speech, given by him in Arabic but followed sentence-by-sentence with an English-translation, he argues that Muslims who have any form of agreement with the UK government (for instance, if they have a UK visa) are prohibited from carrying out attacks within Britain. He adds that there is an additional form of 'customary' or informal contract which prohibits Muslims from attacking their colleagues, employers or people they have exchanged

59 http://forum.islambase.co.uk/index.php?showtopic=2985

60 http://forum.islambase.co.uk/index.php?showtopic=1650&st=40

61 http://islambase.co.uk/index.php?option=com_content&task=category&sectionid=3 3&id=50&Itemid=181

62 http://www.jamestown.org/terrorism/news/article.php?articleid=2370233&printthi s=1

63 http://www.aawsat.com/english/news.asp?section=1&id=1427

greetings with. He gives students studying in the UK as an example:

> "[36:15] Similarly a person who is a student at university, you don't say to the university: 'I'm going to take a covenant of security with you; I'm not going to kill anyone' – people will be shocked if you said that. But it is customary that a person who is a student is not a fighter; the deal in a society where you're studying and you're in the university is that you don't have to take an akuul al-amana [contract/treaty] from them; rather, by you being there; the whole foundation of you being a student means that you're not a fighter; so by being in that situation you have taken a contract of studying with them means that you have a contract with them and you can't betray that."[64]

Tartusi's speech represents an attempt to resurrect the idea of a 'covenant' between Britain and its Muslim inhabitants (not only its citizens) which make jihadist attacks by them *haram*. Islambase users frequently discuss the idea of such a covenant. For example, on 11 August 2007, they discussed whether anti-terrorism arrests had violated Britain's covenant with its Muslims inhabitants – and whether this applied to all Muslims or merely those arrested.[65] (See Appendix III of this report for a longer transcription of al-Tartusi's lecture).

However, in another lecture available on the Islambase website, al-Tartusi defends hardline salafi understandings of the doctrine of takfir; a doctrine frequently used by jihadists to legitimise attacks against other Muslims. In the talk 'Gatherings that mock the deen', al-Tartusi (again speaking in Arabic with a translator) said that any Muslim who does not intervene to prevent "mocking or ridiculing" of Islam ceases to become a Muslim:

> "[03:21] I say as follows that the evidences from the Quran and the Sunnah indicate that the person who is sitting amongst people who are mocking or ridiculing the deen without refuting or rejecting them; without standing up and leaving them; without being forced or compelled [sic] to sit with them, if he doesn't have these three excuses, then he takes the same ruling as those that mock the deen, the takfir ruling, and that is that he is a disbeliever."[66]

---

64 http://islambase.co.uk/index.php?option=com_content&task=view&id=577&Itemid=181

65 http://forum.islambase.co.uk/index.php?showtopic=1295&mode=linearplus

66 http://islambase.co.uk/index.php?option=com_content&task=view&id=728&Itemid=181

For Tartusi, there is no contradiction between holding extremist takfiri beliefs and arguing that Muslims legally in the Britain should not carry out jihadist attacks in the UK. Islambase users regularly cite him as one of their favourite speakers. On 25 October 2007, 'Abu Abdur-Rahman' wrote that on the Islambase forum that:

> "Dr Khalid and Sh Abu Baseer have to be the most technical and methodical speakers i have listened to mashaAllah..."[67]

'Hamza' agreed that:

> "People like Sheik Abu Basir and Dr Khalid Khan have a great way of explaning hadith maybe you heard a thousand times but when they give you the understand you are blown away."

Three of al-Tartusi's written works are also available on the tibyan. wordpress.com website which is popular with Islambase users.[68]

Material by other British extremists

In addition to having recordings by high-profile radical speakers, websites popular with Islambase users also contain numerous recordings of talks given by younger, lesser-known radical preachers. In many cases, the talks given by these 'next-generation' radical preachers promote ideas of violent jihad that are little different from those formerly propagated by individuals such as Abu Hamza or Abdullah Faisal.

■ Abu Omar

In the audio recording of a talk 'Al-Jannah' (paradise), which was posted on the swatulislam.com website on 5 February 2008, a speaker identified only as 'Abu Omar' praised martyrs as the "first people to enter paradise":

> "[55:14] The first people to enter paradise will be the martyr, those people who obey allah [swt] and those poor people who live the life of halal."[69]

---

67 http://forum.islambase.co.uk/index.php?showtopic=1650

68 http://tibyan.wordpress.com/category/abu-basir-at-tartusi/

69 http://www.sawtulislam.com/?p=192

'Abdul Aziz' posted a comment on the talk saying:

"Mashallah! Brilliant talk by Abu Omar. Just to remind everyone that allah has invited us to the gardens of paradise, we would be fools to reject. Subhanallah! oh allah make us all people of jannah. We should all look to ourselves and fix up, we should be engaging in good and forbidding the evil, giving dawah in our societies,culturing the mass, doing the rightous deeds and encouraging those around us, struggling for the deen to be dominent even if it means being boycotted by our communities, being physically or verbally attacked. Brothers and sisters jannah is awaiting us let us be of those who accept this offer. What a wonderfull transaction!"

Paradise and martyrdom are important themes on Islambase-related sites. For example, the tibyan.wordpress.com website, contains a description of paradise written by Ibn al-Qayyim al-Jawziyya (1292-1350AD), a medieval writer popular with modern jihadists:

"And if you ask about what they [inhabitants of paradise] will be hearing, then it is the singing of their wives from among the Hoor al-'Ayn [the maidens of paradise], and better than that are the voices of the Angels and the Prophets, and better than that is the Speech of the Lord of the Worlds. And if you ask about their servants, then they are young boys of everlasting youth who resemble scattered pearls. And if you ask about their brides and wives, then they are young and full-breasted and have had the liquid of youth flow through their limbs; the Sun runs along the beauty of her face if she shows it, light shines from between her teeth if she smiles."[70]

Such descriptions are widely used by jihadists worldwide to portray martyrdom as producing tangible,as well as spiritual, benefits. For instance, in his martyrdom video, Shazad Tanweer, one of the 7 July bombers, addressed British Muslims to remind them of the benefits of paradise, saying:

"You cling inherently to the earth and you believe in the life of this world rather than the hereafter. But little is the enjoyment of this world as compared to the hereafter."[71]

70 http://tibyan.wordpress.com/2007/07/31/description-of-paradise/

71 *The Guardian:* 'Extracts of Tanweer's speech' (15 October 2006) http://www.guardian.co.uk/uk/2006/oct/15/terrorism.alqaida1

■ Abu Sulayman

The sawtulislam.com website hosts several audio recordings by a speaker known as 'Abu Sulayman'. In one talk, 'The Corruption of Western Society', he told listeners that Muslims should be prepared to kill "every single person on earth" in order to eradicate *shirk* (idolatry) which he defines as "the worst type of corruption":

> [12:25] "The worst type of corruption of all is shirk because Muhammad said on his hadiths that it is better for the whole of the earth, every single person on the earth, to be killed than for a single shirk to be prevalent; to be dominant on the earth."[72]

Other parts of the speech attacked Hindus as a source of the "corruption" in British society:

> "[25:57] Hindus are – you wouldn't call it institutionally racist – they are like religiously racist because racism is part of their religion. They have this caste-system where people are grouped depending on who they were born to and they are deliberately discriminated against according to that. So some people have taken that along and even amongst the Ummah they practice this racism."

In addition, however, Abu Sulayman also listed homosexuality, democracy and personal freedom as forms of "corruption" which he wishes to see eradicated:

> "[27:45] I've mentioned racism. What are the other types of corruption? You've got homosexuality, you've got democracy, you've got this whole issue around Hollywood and Bollywood – this whole glamour thing – it's got various branches, pornography, nudity, free-mixing; trying to pass the Kufr culture, trying to get the Muslim children and the Muslim men and women to behave like the Americans; to be shameless."

In another speech, 'Battle of Hattin', Abu Sulayman, describes the battle which was fought in 1187 between the Crusader Kingdom of Jerusalem and a Muslim army led by Salahuddin [Saladin]. Although the talk is mostly a straightforward narrative of the battle and the events leading up to it, he tells his audience that they should compare the era of the Crusades with the modern period:

---

72 http://www.sawtulislam.com/?p=206

"[06: 41] My dear brothers and sisters, I can assure you there is nothing different between what happened in those two hundred years and what is happening today in Iraq, Afghanistan and Palestine and other places. And as we go through this talk, inshallah, I invite you to think for yourself and compare what you hear in the news and what you know from Muslims what is happening in Palestine today and what we are going to talk about today inshallah. Compare and you will see that only the year and the date has been changed."[73]

He also sought to draw out further comparisons between medieval Islamic soldiers and the modern era, saying that the Christian Crusaders had better technology but they lacked willingness to fight and become martyrs:

"[39:45] Many Muslims died – may Allah accept them as shaheed ... [39:59] The Muslims, they are more eager to die to the sake of Allah than the Christians. This is why the RAF pilots were asked by the government 'would you fly suicide missions?' – I bet you they said 'no'."

He also compared the medieval Crusader states to modern-day Israel and said he hoped the young Muslims in the audience will emulate Salahuddin and other medieval Muslim leaders:

"[45:36] That [1291AD] was the end of the 200 years of their occupation of Palestine. Until of course, again we have now Palestine has been occupied for 50 years by the Jews with the backings of the Christians. So this is the current Crusade and we still have to deal with that. We are still waiting for a Salauddin Ayoubi [and also lists other medieval Islamic leaders]... [46:06] We ask Allah to make them rise from the youth that we see in front of us today; from the young children that we see sit here today, to arise leaders like these brave Muslims heroes." [46.15]

He ended his talk by saying:

"[46:20] I finish here, inshallah, a little quote or a little news. They say that when Salauddin Ayoubi after the battle of Hittin, the number of prisoners taken and then the cities and Jerusalam captured, the number the number of prisoners taken [meant] that the Christian slave price was so low that one Muslim soldier exchanged a Christian for an old pair of shoes. This was the izza [honour] that Salauddin Ayoubi brought to the Muslim Ummah."

---

73 http://www.sawtulislam.com/?p=180

27

This speech is a good example of how many British extremists now seek to promote violence without falling foul of laws against inciting violence or glorifying terrorism. Indeed, after recounting the deeds of famous Muslim warriors, Abu Sulayman specifically says that he is not "glorifying" terrorism, even as he says that Muslim capture of the Crusader city of Edessa (a town in present day South-Eastern Turkey) in 1144 AD was comparable to the 11 September attacks:

"[19:27] Now some might say 'incitement', 'glorification' – but let's look at it historically; look at the facts – we don't have to glorify anything."

■ *Abu Uthman*

Abu Uthman is another next-generation extremist speaker whose talks are often recorded and made available on the sawtulislam website. In one talk, 'Steps Towards Conquest of Mekkah', he attacks democracy as "man-made law" and said that non-Muslims were promoting "corruption".[74] He urged his audience to struggle against western influences and to actively reject modern-day corruption such as democracy, describing "Hindus, Sikhs, Jews, Christians" as actively seeking to tempt Muslims away from Islam:

[08:00]So you find at the time of Lut [the prophet Lot] not only were they mushriqs [idolaters] but they were also homosexual. So today we find the same thing don't you? Those people – Hindus, Sikhs, Jews, Christians, you name it. Not only are they mushriq but they're involved in all of the corruption that you can name. Go outside in the streets; go to Bethnal Green, go to Walthamstow. You can see Christians, they've got their ministries and their churches next to nightclubs. You can see that when they talk to people or give talks, there's a woman next to them – they're free-mixing. When a woman sings in the streets – you hear it a lot – they drum down their kufr into your ears and it's a woman singing; they have no shame and *ghira* [jealousy]."

Having urged listeners to reject non-Muslim influences he then told them that "Islam came to rule the world" and said that they should not allow Islam to become a personal or pietistic religion which existed only in mosques:

[11.46] "Many people might say, for example 'why can't the Muslims be con-

---

74 When these sawtulislam.com website was last accessed on 29 April 2008, this talk had been taken offline.

tent and satisfied with living in Medina. Why did they have to spread? What was their problem? Ok. You believe in your belief, Muslims – stay in Medina – why do you want to spread it outside the borders?' The answer to this is very simple; Islam didn't come as a multiple choice questionnaire my dear brothers and sisters, it didn't come as some kind of flavour that if you like the taste of it, you take it and if you don't, you discard it. Islam came to rule the world, Islam came to come and remove the munqer, to remove all the corruption from the face of the earth. But, hamdulillah, if you don't chose to become Muslim fair enough [in Arabic he quotes from the Quran: "Let there be no compulsion in religion"] but you cannot accept for us to live under the man-made law, you cannot accept for us to live under the United Nations resolutions which makes everyone equal in the eyes of man when we say Islam is superior and nothing can supercede it. So this is our objective, my dear Muslims, when we analyse the way the prophet took over the Arabian Peninsula it reminds us that, yes, he commanded good and he forbade evil. Yes, he gave dawa on an individual level and a collective level. But that was all for an objective … [13:35] the objective that is har al-din; that we one day want to see in the UK [13.39] the black flag of Islam over Ten Downing Street. That we're not happy to stay in our mosques talking about iman [faith] and yakeen [faith] – talking about something that hamdullilah [praise be to God] is good but is does not achieve the objective that we are trying to achieve. [13.55]"

Other parts of the talk similarly depict Muhammad as having an expansionist, imperialist vision of Islam.

[39:38] "He [Muhammad] wasn't content. His eyes, my dear Muslims, were on the whole world; his eyes, my dear Muslims were on conquering the Roman empire, the Persian empire, America, Britain, Australia – you name it. That was the vision of the messenger."

■ **Abu Ibrahim**

One of the most regularly featured speakers on Islambase is Abu Ibrahim. The website hosts 68 audio recordings of his talks.[75] He is also one of the most aggressive speakers and his talks indicate how modern extremists aim to incite violence and hatred through citing historical examples of Muslim committing violence in the name of Islam and promoting theologies that argue that Muslims are have an obligation to fight and conquer non-Muslims – rather than explicitly calling

---

75 http://islambase.co.uk/index.php?option=com_content&task=category&sectionid=3 3&id=47&Itemid=181

for attacks. In his lecture, "I have been ordered to fight", Abu Ibrahim told his audience that Muslims are obliged to fight non-Muslims until they accept Islam or agree to live as second-class citizens under Muslim rule.

In particular he told his audience that it is the duty of Muslims:

> "[11:00] to fight the people until they testify that there is none worth of worship but Allah and that Muhammad is his messenger".

He emphasised that all and "any" people should be fought regardless of their religion:

> "[10:44] He [God] doesn't just say [fight] the mushrikeen [idolators], he doesn't just say the yehud [Jews] and he doesn't say the polytheists, the idol-worshippers or the yehud, the jews, or the nasara [Christians]; he doesn't say any of these things, he says 'any people'".

He also said that Muslims should not become "apologetic" about Islam's violent history or reject violent aspects of Islam:

> "[11:34] Many people, when they write history, they have a problem also to say that Islam was spread by the sword. People like to think it was just a way of invitation [i.e. conversion], that there was no sword involved; no fighting involved. Why? Because many people feel embarrassed because the kuffar put it in the heads of the Muslims that how can you be someone who is preaching the word of God, God who is most merciful, most kind and yet you talk about the fact that he needed to raise a sword ... [25:11]this is the way that the shaytan [devil/followers of the devil] twist things. That's why as Muslims we should be firm in our knowledge of Islam ... [12:45] If they say that the history of Islam is barbaric, so be it – that be your opinion, it is not for us. We know that Islam had a glorious history and yes, the Rasool [the messenger. i.e. Muhammad] took up arms; he had a spear; in fact he said, 'my provisions from Allah is the shadow of my spear, below the shadow of my sword'. Why? Because he was someone Muslim. He was someone who said 'look, I am being commanded to fight the people until they submit' And he is our example for us to follow."

In the same talk, he discussed how Muhammad himself had treated apostates from Islam:

> "[19:32] [Apostates were] fought, captured and then the capital punishment applied upon them. They were nailed to a stake and the rasool [Muhammad],

he cut one hand off, one feet off and even put nails through their eyes. Why? Because he was commanded by Allah to fight these people. Fight them until they say *there is no prophet but Allah and Muhammad is his messenger* [Arabic]. Once you give up on this then you become a people who it is eligible to fight against."

He repeats that Islam obligates fighting non-Muslims until Islam becomes "dominant" over them or until they convert to Islam:

"[20:08] We need to understand that part and parcel of Islam is the fact that we struggle for the sake of Allah [swt]; to make Islam dominant; to spread it. So the rasool said "fight a people until they say *'there is no god but Allah and Muhammad is his prophet'* [in Arabic]."

He added that if non-Muslims refuse to convert, they can agree to live under Muslim rule and pay the *jiyza* (a poll tax levied only on non-Muslims). But he said that if they refuse, then Muslim armies should continue to fight them until their opponents are killed:

"[41:54] If you [non-Muslims] don't want to embrace Islam then give still the haq of Allah, the haq ['truth'] of Islam, which is the jiyza. And if the people were to do this ... [42:25] If you do this then again the Muslim army moves on; it leaves someone in authority. The kuffar cannot be in authority – even if everyone there is a kafir, the one who is in governance, the one who is in authority must be a Muslim. Islam is superior and nothing else is more superior than it. And thereafter, if the people refused it, then we have the words of Khalid bin Waleed; 'I bring with me a people who love death the way you love life'."

The ideas that Muslims should love death and should fight until the world is ruled by Islam play an important role in jihadist ideology. Osama bin Laden, speaking shortly after the 11 September attacks told Hamid Mir, a Pakistani journalist, that "We love death. The U.S. loves life. That is the big difference between us."[76] Similarly, in 2003, the Madrid bombers made recordings in which they warned Spain that "You love life and we love death".[77]

---

76 *Time* magazine: 'Osama bin Laden and the idea of progress', Richard Stengel. 21 December 2001. http://www.time.com/time/columnist/stengel/article/0,9565,189648,00.html

77 Jamestown Foundation: 'The Madrid bombings: Spain as a jihad highway to western Europe' by John C K Daly. 15 March 2004. http://www.jamestown.org/terrorism/news/article.php?issue_id=2921

■ *Abu Mujahidah*

The Islambase website also includes eight talks by 'Abu Mujahidah'. His talks usually aim to create a sense of persecution and victimhood among his Muslim audience. For example, in one talk entitled 'Wisdom and Testing', 'Abu Mujahidah' said:

> "[4:29] We see that the Muslims are losing more land, the Muslims are losing more of their government, we see that the Muslims are losing more of their unity, and it is the kuffar that is getting the upper hand. It is the kuffar, the non-Muslims, the disbelievers, who take more authority on the earth, on the world, than the Muslims are. And all we have to do is turn on the TV and watch Gordon Brown. This week, where he went to America to firm his alliance with this shayatan [devil], Bush. And at the same time, he went to the United Nations, the first thing he did in the United Nations was to say that they are to deal with this situation in Darfur...we see wherever the kuffar goes, he or she, they go for a reason. They go for a purpose, and they go for something materialistic."[78]

Talks such as these arguably play a key role in persuading British Muslims that non-Muslims are constantly plotting against them. Other talks given by Mujahidah have a similar them. In a talk 'Kosovo', he describes attacks on Muslims in Yugoslavia, while in another 'Who is the terrorist?', he describes US policy in Pakistan, British counter-terrorism policy and European colonialism as being different aspects of Western hostility to Islam.[79]

On 26 October 2007, in a discussion on the Islambase forum, the administrator of the sawtulislam website cited Abu Mujahidah as one of his favourite speakers.[80]

---

78 http://islambase.co.uk/index.php?option=com_content&task=category&sectionid=3 3&id=135&Itemid=181

79 http://islambase.co.uk/index.php?option=com_content&task=view&id=1096&Itemi d=181]

80 http://forum.islambase.co.uk/index.php?showtopic=1650&hl=Abu%20Mujahidah &st=20]

■ *Abu Osama*

In addition to hosting audio-recordings of talks, Islambase also hosts documents apparently written by British-based extremists. For example, the site contains a PDF copy of 'Voting in Democratic Elections: The Islamic Ruling concerning its participation' by 'Abu Osama'. This 13-page pamphlet says that democracy is un-Islamic and that it is not permissible for Muslims to take part in any aspects of the democratic process:

> "If we truly look to Islam we can now see that it is strictly forbidden to vote let alone believe in the system of democracy. To even have the notion that certain parties are good gives weight to the views that there is a choice in command as to what we are allowed to live by as such as man made laws. At the end of the day democracy is a system put in replacement of Shari'ah and no matter which party goes through the issues such as homosexuality, pornography, alcoholism, relaxed drug laws, nudity, promiscuity, Adultery, fornication, gambling, pop culture, Interest and inflation will never be an issue as they consider it their social values and as we know these are things forbidden in Islam."[81]

Another work by Abu Osama is 'The Plague of the West' which is available on Islambase as a PDF.[82] The introductory chapter reads:

> "This short work has been compiled to expose the fallacy of the Western nations and the culture and civilisation they profess to believe in and live by. Its aim is to educate those in the Muslim world the true picture of life in the Western countries with a view to demolish the myth that the west has the solution to all the world's problems. Rather the West is the cause and source of all the worlds' problems!"[83]

The work then goes on to attack secularism, democracy, freedom, liberalism, human rights and other ideas as the "the founding principles which the western nations pride themselves on", before attacking "single-parent families", "sexual deviancy" and "paedophilia" as an inevitable outcome of Western ideas, saying that:

---

81 http://downloads.islambase.co.uk/books/Voting.pdf (p. 12)

82 http://downloads.islambase.co.uk/books/PlagueWest.pdf

83 http://downloads.islambase.co.uk/books/PlagueWest.pdf p.1

33

"Such is the availability of sexual material, be it films, magazines or internet sites that people are not able to satisfy their satanic appetites and lusts; as a consequence, rape, homosexuality and paedophilia the sexual abuse of children and often babies have become rampant." [p. 16]

He then writes about "western women":

"Sexually denigrated, alcoholic and drug dependent, abused, attacked and raped, constant thoughts of suicide and self harm, deeply depressed, pandering after equality such is the nature of the liberated Western woman!" [p. 18]

The publication ends with a call for Sharia to be adopted in the UK as the only solution to the problems listed by the author, describing it as "a complete way of life affording practical and lasting solutions to the Western problems." (p. 40).

A similar PDF-publication by Abu Anas, apparently another member of the Islambase circle, entitled 'Multi-Cultural Society or Racist Society' makes similar points, telling readers that Islam is the solution to racism. The writer additionally attacks government attempts to encourage Muslim integration which he depicts as part of a broader, long-standing war against Islam:

"There is an ongoing campaign launched by the kuffar which aims to remedy the problem that the west faces with Islam. The kuffar have tried physically forcing the Muslims to change in the past but failed in doing so, hence their strategy has been adapted. There is currently being waged upon the Muslims a campaign to remove their Islamic identity by reducing Islam to another fanciful philosophy like Christianity. They desire for Muslims to compromise their beliefs and hold them second in value to all else. They see that the hindrance to progression in the West are the Muslims who carry the banner of Islam, who call for the implementation of Allah (swt)'s law and refuse to accept and abide by the law of man." [p.9]

It is likely that such publications act as supporting material to the many lectures and recording available on the Islambase website by clearly explaining and enlarging upon the themes mentioned by speakers.

CHAPTER 3:

Messages from foreign extremists

Websites popular with Islambase users regularly post and distribute messages and texts by members of al-Qaeda and other related groups. These include propaganda videos and statements issued by Osama bin Laden and Abu Musab al-Zarqawi as well as numerous texts and recordings by lesser-known extremists.

■ Material produced by al-Qaeda

The tibyan.wordpress website which is regularly cited by Islambase users has publicised videos produced by Musab al-Zarqawi's al-Qaeda organisation in Iraq.[84] On 16 August 2007, the website posted links to a video of one of Zarqawi's sermons, stored on www.archive.org, a US-based website. The film contains extensive footage of car bombings, dead civilians and injured American soldiers, over which Zarqawi is heard saying:

> "[24:45] This is Jihad…the pinnacle…and fruits…it comes after a long period of patience and active dwelling in the land of battle, waiting for the roar of the enemies, and withstanding their evil; a dwelling that lasts months and years, continuously one after another. And if you do not gulp these pains, then Allah will not give you victory – because Nasr (Victory) comes with Sabr (patience)."

Although the actual video was stored on www.archive.org, the tibyan website attempted to present it as their own, entitling the blog "The Media Department Of At-Tibyan Publications Presents 'Such Are the Messengers Tested, and Then the Outcome Will Be In Their Favor' … By the Shaykh, the Commander, AbūMus'ab Az-Zarqāwī, (May Allāh have Mercy upon him)".[85]

On 25 January 2008, the tibyan.wordpress.com website posted videos,

---

84 http://tibyan.wordpress.com/category/abu-musab-az-zarqawi/

85 http://tibyan.wordpress.com/2007/08/16/such-are-the-messengers-tested-and-then-the-outcome-will-be-in-their-favor/. The actual video is stored at http://www.archive.org/download/zarqawieidkhutbah/zarqawieidkhutbah1.mpg

audio files and transcripts from an al-Qaeda-produced video 'Escape from Bagram' which detailed the escape of three al-Qaeda members from a US-run prison in Bagram, Afghanistan, in July 2005.[86] The video, produced by Labbayk media, one of the al-Qaeda's main media outlets, shows the three al-Qaeda men describing their escape from the top security prison. It begins with an image of two crossed AK-47 assault rifles and then says that it is dedicated:

"To the Muslims across the world under the oppression of the Kuffar and Tawaghit; to the Muslims to know the promise of Allah is true, and to those deviated Muslims who hearts hold doubts about the power of al-Qawiyy al-Aziz [i.e. God].

The bulk of the recording comprises of interviews with the escapees telling their story and assorted footage of them and other mujahideen in Afghanistan. The video – which has English-subtitles – is offered on the tibyan website in high quality AVI files, low quality Real Media files and even ipod-compatible videos. A written English-language transcript of the video is also available. As with the previous video, Tibyan take credit for the translation of the video, even though they did not produce it.

Similar recordings are also available directly through Islambase. On 8 May 2007, 'khalimat Noor', a regular Islambase user who claims to be a 24-year old woman, added a link to another al-Qaeda propaganda video, 'Badr Ar-Riyadh', which is available at archive.org.[87] The 47-minute video, produced by al-Qaeda's al-Sahab media department, focuses on an attack by the group in Riyadh, Saudi Arabia which killed 18 people on 8 November 2004. Subtitled in English, the video mixed extensive interviews with the al-Qaeda members carried out the attack with excerpts from previous talks by Osama bin Laden and other senior al-Qaeda leaders. The video begins with a graphic of the US flag flying over the Arabian Peninsula which then explodes as an Arabic song begins, subtitled in English:

"[01:00] Blow them up ... blow them up everywhere they are and slay them"[88]

---

86 http://tibyan.wordpress.com/2008/01/25/coming-soon-escape-from-bagram/

87 http://forum.islambase.co.uk/index.php?showtopic=10

88 An extensive transcript of the video is available at the Intel Center http://www.intelcenter.com/Badr-al-Riyadh-v1-1.pdf

While the actual video is stored at archive.org, 'Khalimat Noor' posted screen-grabs from the recording directly onto the Islambase website. The same day, she also posted links to another video stored at archive. org, part one of 'Knights of Martyrdom', a propaganda video produced by Zarqawi's Islamic State of Iraq.[89] The 39-minute video, entirely in Arabic, contains extensive interviews with would-be suicide bombers in Iraq, clips from bin Laden's speeches and music glorifying martyrdom.

■ Material glorifying al-Qaeda and jihadist violence

Several websites recommended by Islambase users contain material glorifying jihadist leaders and their ideas. For example, the Kalamullah. com website hosts recordings of an unidentified British speaker giving a series of talks on 'Heroes of Islam'.[90] One of these recordings describes the life of Abdullah Azzam, the leader of the Arab volunteers who fought the Soviet Army in Afghanistan in the 1990s.[91] In the recording, the speaker praises Azzam as the greatest Muslim of the age:

"[01:05] As Osama bin Laden said, 'Sheikh Abdullah Azzam was not an individual but an entire nation by himself and the Muslim nation has proven themselves incapable of giving birth to a man like him after he was killed'."

The speaker goes on to praise Azzam for carrying out jihad at the expense of other aspects of Islamic practice:

"[23:44] He would say that 'I feel I am only nine years old; seven and a half-years in the Afghan jihad and one-and-a-half years in the jihad of Palestine and the rest of my years have been of no value'. So he's saying no value to the amount of time he spent studying Sharia, to the time he spent giving dawa, to the time he spent gaining his PhD in Sool al-Fiqh [CHECK]. It shows the level of commitment that he reached towards."

Also featured in the 'Heroes of Islam' series is Sayyed Qutb, a member of the Egyptian Muslim Brotherhood (d. 1966) who was arguably the

---

89 http://forum.islambase.co.uk/index.php?showtopic=9&hl=

90 http://www.kalamullah.com/lectures.html

91 http://www.kalamullah.com/Heroes%20Of%20Islam/CD10ShaykhAbdullahAzzam. mp3

leading ideologue of the modern jihadist movement.[92] The recording begins by describing him as a "hero":

> "[00:27] Today we are going to talk about a hero who really has influenced the minds, the thoughts and the ideologies of the major mujahideen around the world and those people that are striving hard in the way of Allah against oppressive regimes. The hero who we are going to talk about today if you ask them they will say they have been influenced directly as a result of this man and his writings. If you ask, for example, Sheikh Abdullah Azzam he would say that the person was most influenced by in his life was [the] shahid [Qutb]."

A "bonus track" on the Kalamullah website's 'Heroes on Islam' section features Tamim al-Adnan, one of the leading members of the "Arab-Afghans", the Muslim volunteers who fought the USSR in Afghanistan.[93] In the recording, made sometime, in the US in the late-1980s, he tells his audience:

> "[02:41] One of the greatest chances to go to Jannah in the month of Ramadan is jihad. We are the nation of jihad. Jihad is one of the main fards [obligations] of Islam that Allah has ordered us to perform."

Websites popular with Islambase users also contain pro-jihadist material from the 1980s and 1990s. For example, the Kalamullah website contains a recording of 'In the Hearts of the Green Birds: The martyrs of Bosnia', a recording produced in the 1990s which eulogises "martyrs" killed in the Bosnian wars. The recording says in its introduction that it contains:

> "[00.25] Real life experiences in jihad and on inspiring accounts of the shohadat [martyrs]; of those brothers killed in the way of Allah."[94]

The recording itself consists of dramatic accounts of the lives and deaths of individual mujahideen, interspersed with martial music and sounds of gunfire. Many of the accounts feature quasi-mystical stories of the mujhaideen receiving divine assistance, descriptions of acts of extreme heroism in the cause of jihad and the Muslim fighters eagerly embracing martyrdom.

---

92 http://www.kalamullah.com/Heroes%20Of%20Islam/CD8SyedQutub.mp3

93 http://www.kalamullah.com/Tamim%20Adnani/Sheilkh%20Tamim%20Adnani.mp3

94 http://www.kalamullah.com/others/In_the_Hearts_of_Green_Birds.mp3

The website also contains an mp3 of 'Under the Shade of Swords', a sequel to 'Green Birds' which contains further details of other mujahideen killed in Bosnia. The two recordings were originally produced and distributed in cassette form by London-based Azzam Publications. According to the US government, Azzam Publications was allegedly part-run by Babar Ahmad, a British Muslim who is presently fighting extradition to the US on charges of "conspiring to support terrorism".[95]

On several occasions, individuals have posted extracts from 'In the hearts of Green Birds' on Islambase forums. On 13 April 2007, 'Umm Khalid, a woman, posted a partial transcript of the 'Green Birds' recording which describes the life and death of a Kuwaiti volunteer fighter in Bosnia. She prefaces the extract by saying:

> "Subhanallah...its a very touching story...its never too late to share it out with the rest i hope it touches every persons heart who reads it inshallah...as it has done to me..."[96]

The story describes the man's death, recounting that his "soul left his body with a clearly distinct smile on his face" and saying that dead man appeared in the dreams of other mujahideen and described to them the delights of paradise. One Islambase user, 'Abdulrahman al muhajir', responded to the story by writing "mashallah beautifull story may allah accept fom amongst the shuhada" [marytrs].[97] The idea of Muslim martyrs travelling to heaven "in the hearts of green birds" has been used in poetry by Samina Malik, 'the lyrical terrorist', in her poem 'Fear No Man – Fear Allah', she wrote:

> "Who will show us the Light and Reward us in the Hearts of Green Birds in the Highest of Jannah'"[98]

In 2008, Malik was found guilty under the 2006 Terrorism Act and received a nine-month suspended prison sentence for "collecting in-

---

95 *BBC:* 'Babar set to fight extradition'. 16 November 2005. http://news.bbc.co.uk/1/hi/uk/4441448.stm

96 http://forum.islambase.co.uk/index.php?showtopic=166&hl=green+birds

97 http://forum.islambase.co.uk/index.php?showtopic=166&hl=green+birds

98 http://freesaminamalik.blogspot.com/2007/11/poetry-cannot-be-arrest.html

formation, without reasonable excuse, of a kind likely to be useful to a person committing or preparing an act of terrorism".[99]

■ Abu Mohammad Al-Maqdisi

The Islambase site contains several works by Abu Muhammad al-Maqdisi (Isam Muhammad Tahir al-Barqawi) in the section 'Books in English' which is listed on the website's homepage as one of its five most popular pages. [100]Al-Maqdisi, a Jordanian, is one of the world's leading jihadi scholars and is credited with radicalising Abu Musab al-Zarqawi during time the two spent in prison together in the 1990s.

The Islambase website holds three PDF version's of Maqdisi's *Millet Ibrahim* ("The Faith of Abraham"); two copies in English and one in Bengali.[101] According to *Asharq al-Awsat*, the pan-Arab newspaper, this book "is similar to Sayyid Qutb's *Milestones* in terms of its impact on Salafi ideology."[102] One Islambase user, 'Musafir', described Millet Ibrahim as one of his favourites books .[103]

PDF versions of another of Maqdisi's books, *Democracy: A religion*, are also available on the Islambase and salafiyyah-jadeedah websites. This book is one of the most important modern works on jihad. The book seeks to persuade the reader that a Muslim who believes in democracy thereby makes himself a "kuffar" or unbeliever. Those who support the "man-made" system of democracy, Maqdisi says, should be killed and he urges

> "Jihad against the deity, his followers, and helpers, to try to damage this man-made system, and to try to get the people to turn away from worshipping it and return to the worship of Allah alone."

---

99 *BBC:* Terror manuals woman avoids jail (6 December 2007) http://news.bbc.co.uk/1/hi/uk/7130495.stm

100 http://islambase.co.uk/index.php?option=com_content&task=view&id=510&Itemid=171

101 http://islambase.co.uk/index.php?option=com_content&task=view&id=510&Itemid=171

102 *Asharq al-Awsat:* Abu Mohammed al Maqdisi: al-Zarqawi's "Spiritual Godfather" By Mshari Al-Zaydi (26 July 2005) http://aawsat.com/english/news.asp?section=3&id=968

103 http://forum.islambase.co.uk/index.php?showtopic=811

Maqdisi's book *This Is Our Aqeedah* (available in PDF form on Islambase and tibyan.wordpress.com) similarly justifies violence against all who seek to tempt Muslims away from salafist versions of Islam.[104] One Islambase reader, 'al-Mansoer' described the book in March 2007 as "a must-read!!".[105]

Islambase users also use the website to distribute Maqdisi's more obscure works. On 9 May 2007, 'abdulrahman al muhajir' posted a short article by Maqdisi entitled 'The Caravan is Moving and the Dogs are Barking'.[106] The article attacks those who seek to undermine jihadist ideologies and tells jihadists to ignore all criticism and continue their attacks:

> "[And] You, good Mujahideen, the best answer to those bad people is ignoring them and to stay with the Jihad and to continue to kill and fight every enemy of Allaah."

The article also says that those Muslims who seek to prevent jihad are committing a worse crime than any jihadists who accidentally kills innocent Muslims:

> "The crime of stopping the jihad is much bigger than any crime that they accuse the Mujahideen of committing. If the Mujahideen make a mistake they do not need feedback from the infidels because they know better than anybody else what is right and what is wrong."

On 1 March 2008, 'Hamza' posts a fresh link to this article and wrote:

> "I have never in my life read anything written by any man of my generation as much as this. When all else fails i just have to read this for things to make sense again."[107]

'Abu Hamza al-Britani' agreed, writing "subhan Allah, what an amazing article."

---

104 http://tibyan.wordpress.com/2007/08/24/this-is-our-%e2%80%98aqidah/ and http://islambase.co.uk/index.php?option=com_content&task=view&id=510&Itemid=1 71

105 http://forum.islambase.co.uk/index.php?showtopic=15

106 http://forum.islambase.co.uk/index.php?showtopic=249&hl

107 http://forum.islambase.co.uk/index.php?showtopic=2694&hl=maqdisi

Many users of Islambase share his high opinion. On 17 June 2007, another Islambase reader, 'Abdulrahman al muhajir', responded to news that Maqdisi has on hunger-strike by writing "May Alllah release the shaykh and strenghten his imaan insha'allah".[108] On 15 March 2008, 'Abumusab' posted the news that al-Maqdisi had been released from prison in Jordan by writing that:

> "Sheikh muhammud al maqdisi released, a bit late but still da best news in ages."

On many occasions, Islambase users share and distribute Maqdisi's texts among themselves.. On 15 August 2007, 'Adil_11_1', who said he already had three Maqdisi books, wrote on the Islambase forum "if anyone has links to books by abu muhammad al maqdisi can you please post them up".[109] Three users responded to his request by sending him links to several websites where online copies of Maqdisi's books are available.

This shows how the Islambase website plays an important role in helping British extremists to find and distribute pro-jihadist texts which may otherwise be hard to track down. Islambase's books page has more works by Maqdisi than any other scholar.[110] It includes two different English editions of his books *Millet Ibrahim* and one in Bengali as well as two different editions of *This Is Our Aqeedah*. The salafiyyah-jadeedah website, popular with Islambase users, also contains another work attacking secularism by al-Maqdisi. entitled 'Believe in Allah and Disbelieve in Taaghoot' [tyranny].[111]

■ Yusuf al-Ayyari

Websites popular with Islambase users contain a large amount of material by Sheikh Yusuf al-Ayyari (his surname is also spelt al-Ayeri, Uyyari or al-Uyayri), who was a leading member of al-Qaeda's network

---

108 http://forum.islambase.co.uk/index.php?showtopic=467

109 http://forum.islambase.co.uk/index.php?showtopic=1335

110 http://islambase.co.uk/index.php?option=com_content&task=view&id=510&Itemid=171

111 http://salafiyyah-jadeedah.tripod.com/Legislation/Disbelieve_in_Taaghoot.htm

in Saudi Arabia before he was killed by Saudi security forces in June 2003.[112]

The Islambase website contains his book 'The Ruling on Jihad and its Divisions' by "Sheikh Yusuf al-Ayaari", which appears to have been translated by Abu Usama specifically for Islambase. This short work is a straightforward call for violent jihad, summarising references to jihad in the Quran, the hadiths and citing major Islamic scholars such as ibn Qayyim and Imam Qurbuti who, he believed, argued that jihad is an "important Divine obligation" which should be carried out to spread Islam:

> "The obligation of Jihad will only ever cease being a duty when Jihad's true purpose is realised, that being the complete control of the whole earth such that not a single hand-span is left which is not under Islamic rule or by struggling ones utmost to accomplish this. Only when this has been done, does the obligation of Jihad cease since the Muslims have tried their best to realise its aims and objectives and Allah (swt) does not burden a soul more than it can bear."[113] (p.7)

Al-Ayyari attacks arguments that jihad is only ever a defensive act:

> "Some of those who assert themselves to be scholars and people of knowledge – and in fact have been made blind by Allah (swt) – claim that there is only Defensive Jihad in Islam. As a consequence they work to distort the statements of the Scholars and the Islamic texts to negate the obligation of Offensive Jihad and fighting the disbelievers in their homelands ... other so-called scholars falsely claim that all the battles that the Prophet (saw) fought were Defensive in nature."[114] (p. 8)

The tibyan.wordpress website also contains English translations of four other works by al-Ayyari.[115] One book, 'The Role of Women in Fighting the Enemies', explains how Muslim women are presently "one of the biggest impediments before the victory and honour of Islam" by preventing their menfolk from taking part in fighting but that they should

---

112 *Jamestown Foundation:* 'A guide to jihad on the web' by Stephen Ulph (31 March 2005) http://www.jamestown.org/terrorism/news/article.php?articleid=2369531

113 http://downloads.islambase.co.uk/books/RulingJihad.pdf

114 http://downloads.islambase.co.uk/books/RulingJihad.pdf

115 http://tibyan.wordpress.com/category/yusuf-ibn-salih-al-%e2%80%98uyayri/

instead encourage men to take part in the jihad and even take part in fighting themselves. Elsewhere on the Islambase site, Omar Bakri describes al-Ayyari as "a great fighter, a lion of Islam".[116]

■ Other salafi-jihadist writers

In addition to having online copies of materials produced by members of al-Qaeda and other extreme jihadist organisations, Islambase also hosts a number of books by lesser known writers – as do several other websites cited by Islambase users.

For instance, the Islambase website hosts a copy of 'In Pursuit of Allah's Pleasure', co-authored by Dr Najeh Ibrahim, Asim Abdul-Majid and Esaam ud-Deen Darbaalah of Egypt's Islamic Jihad group. First published in 1984, the book was the inspiration for many jihadists in the 1980s. It advocates purifying Islamic societies of non-Muslim influences in order to re-create the Caliphate and apply Sharia law. Like many books popular with jihadists, the book emphasises the need to take action against Muslim secularists:

> "Our fortresses are threatened from within because we have allowed contradictory and deviant creeds and ideologies to share them with us and they have undermined our very structure. Our fortresses are crowded and falling apart, unable to withstand the blows of the enemies, let alone prepare us for mounting an attack. Our advice to our fellow Muslims is that we must hasten to clear our fortresses from those who have been causing this confusion." (p. 142-3)

Although nearly 25 years old, the book is still seen as relevant by some Islambase users. For example, on 2 June 2007, a guest on the Islambase forum asked for an online copy of the book and was directed to the site's online library.[117]

Similarly, several texts on the salafiyyah-jadeedah website aim to justify jihadist violence. For example, the website contains a fatwa issued by Shaykh Muhammad Aal 'Abd al-Lateef, a Saudi cleric, in response to

---

116 01:10, http://islambase.co.uk/index.php?option=com_content&task=view&id=401&Itemid=181

117 http://forum.islambase.co.uk/index.php?showtopic=289

a petitioner who asks whether an individual can carry out jihad when there is no caliphate:

Question: Can we really participate in Jihaad when we don't have any khalifa to organise us, or we don't have the strength to fight them? Do we behave like the Prophet (SM) did having patience and trust in Allah (S) before gaining the strength to fight the kuffar?

Answer: Praise be to Allaah. Jihaad for the sake of Allaah is the pinnacle of Islam, and is one of the principles of the religion. It does not depend on there being an imaam (khaleefah or ruler)... But obviously jihaad requires preparation and organization, and the existence of a leader of the army who can weigh up the pros and cons. This strikes the balance between those who are reckless and pay no attention to the regulations of sharee'ah [sharia], and those who neglect this duty and ignore it completely. It is obligatory to follow the example of the Prophet (peace and blessings of Allaah be upon him) in all his affairs, which includes preparation and equipping oneself.[118]

Fatwas such as these are critical in giving religious legitimacy to the idea that jihad can be undertaken by individuals whether or not they have the backing of religious authorities or of a recognised Islamic ruler.

Readers of such material who wish to know more about carrying out jihad can easily find it. The tibyan.wordpress.com hosts a PDF copy of the book '39 Ways to Serve and Participate in Jihad' by Muhammad bin Ahmad as-Sālim (also known as 'Isā al-'Awshin).[119] The ways listed in the book include to "collect funds for the mujahidin", "call and incite the people to jihad" and "have enmity towards the Disbelievers and hate them". In the section 'Raise your children to love jihad and its people', as-Salim writes:

"One's family and children are the preparation for the future and are them-selves the future generation, so it is a must to raise one's family and children upon the love of jihad and the mujahidin, and the concepts of martyrdom and sacrifice for the Religion of Allah." [page. 46]

Salih suggests that this can be done by "bringing to them tapes (both

---

118 http://salafiyyah-jadeedah.tripod.com/Qital/Imam_condition.htm

119 http://tibyan.wordpress.com/2007/08/24/39-ways-to-serve-and-participate-in-jihad/ (nb. the PDF of this tibyan publication is stored at www.archive.org, a US-based website. The tibyan website provides a direct link to the article.

video and audio) of the mujahidin so that they would increase in their love of jihad and attachment to the mujahidin" and "naming one's children after the past and present heroes of jihad." (p. 47)

Another popular writer is Abdullah Azzam, one of the leaders of the Arab mujahideen who fought against the USSR in Afghanistan in the 1980s and was a mentor to Osama bin Laden. Sites such as tibyan. wordpress.com and Islambase frequently distribute Azzam's texts and writings – many of which explicitly call for armed jihad against non-Muslims. For example, on 10 April 2008, 'Hamza' posted a short piece by Azzam entitled 'Learning to Use Weapons is from the Way of the Salaf'. The article tells readers that:

> "So the Lord of Honour has obligated preparation with a weapon and a horse to affront the enemies of Allâh and humiliate them." [120]

British terrorism prosecutors have frequently used possession of Azzam's books and articles as evidence that individuals are planning acts of violence. For example, in July 2007, five men from Bradford were convicted of possessing extremist material downloaded from websites.[121] Although they were later freed on appeal, all five men were found to possess downloaded copies of Azzam's book 'Join the Caravan'. [122]

The salafiyyah-jadeedah.tripod.com website contains a lengthy article called 'Jihad – a 10 part compliation' which seeks to combine the teachings of different jihadist authors.[123] Based around the 'Defence of Muslim Lands: The first obligation after Imaan [faith]' by Abdullah Azzam, it includes excerpts from other jihadist writers to strengthen Azzam's arguments where necessary and to address subjects which he did not directly refer to. Thus, while the compilation uses as its framework Azzam's teachings that jihad can be conducted without a caliph and that jihad is an obligatory "an act of worship" which should be undertaken to free Muslim lands from non-Muslim occupation, these teachings are

---

120 http://forum.islambase.co.uk/index.php?showtopic=3351&st=0&p=17295&#entry 17295

121 Crown Prosecution Service. Press release: 'Five men sentenced for possessing extremist material' 26 July 2007.

122 *BBC:* 'Students who descended into extremism'. 26 July 2007. http://news.bbc. co.uk/1/hi/uk/6916654.stm

123 http://salafiyyah-jadeedah.tripod.com

MESSAGES FROM FOREIGN EXTREMISTS

supplements by even more radical ideas. Thus the compilation includes one fatwa by Sheikh Muhammed Salih Al-Munajjid, a Saudi Salafi scholar, outlining the conditions under which Muslim women can take up arms and another by Hasan Abi'l-Ghuddah, another Saudi cleric, saying that prisoners of war can be killed if necessary.[124] In support of this, the compilation's authors quote from 'The Story of the 600-700 Jews Beheaded by the Prophet (SAWS) at Bani Quraiza in 5 AH" from 'The Sealed Nectar', a popular biography of Muhammad.[125] This story recounts Muhammad's execution of the male members of the Jewish tribe Banu Qurayza in 627 AD and concludes that by this action "Hot beds [sic] of intrigue and treachery were thus exterminated once and for all". The compilation also contains excepts from 'The Absent Obligation', a book by Muhammad Abd al-Salam Faraj, whose followers assassinated Anwar Sadat, the Egyptian president in 1981 in which he tells readers to fight rather than accumulate Islamic knowledge:

> "Knowledge is not the sharp and striking weapon that will cut the roots of the disbelievers."[126]

The salafiyyah-jadeedah.tripod website's 'Jihad – a 10 part compliation' illustrates the dangers of the internet. The compilation's authors – who are anonymous – have simply collected the most violent and aggressive Islamic texts available on the internet, crudely spliced them together and then published the result online.

---

124 http://salafiyyah-jadeedah.tripod.com/Qital/Part_3.htm, http://salafiyyah-jadeedah.tripod.com/Qital/Part_9.htm.

125 http://salafiyyah-jadeedah.tripod.com/Qital/Part_9.htm

126 http://salafiyyah-jadeedah.tripod.com/Qital/Part_5.htm

CHAPTER 4:

Nasheeds

Several of the websites popular with Islambase users contain considerable numbers of Nasheeds, traditional Arabic songs which usually address religious issues. In particular, Islambase itself and sawtulislam, host dozens of Nasheeds which glorify Islamic violence and attacks against Israelis, the West and Muslims who are opposed to the jihadist movement. Although these Nasheeds are mostly in Arabic which severely limits their potential audience among British Muslims in general, evidence from elsewhere on the websites suggest that many readers of Islambase and other sites have learnt or are learning Arabic.

Extracts from Arabic nasheeds on the sawtulislam website:[127]

Qom (A Stand):
(Audio only)

> [0:29] *With machine guns we have returned to own the day of reckoning in groups and individually*
> *The only thing we know in life is violence*
>
> [02:35] *You oppressors, you evil doers, you waste of time; the day of reckoning has arrived, as we have come for you with our automatic guns [machine gun sound] and our holy Quran.*

Irhaabiyyun Anaa (I am a terrorist):
(Audio only)

> *We are terrorists and terror is our path*
> *The East and West needs to know that we are terrorists,*
> *Fearsome terrorists using everything in our power*
> *And all the horses we have*
> *To fight the enemy of Prophet Muhammad, your enemy and the enemies of God.*
>
> *I am a terrorist terrorising the enemy of the deen.*

---

127 http://www.sawtulislam.com/?page_id=43

49

> *With the sword, with fire we scare the enemy*
> *And the lord will make the pure-warriors victorious.*
> *[They] have killed you, backstabbed you, oppressed you...*
> *The day is coming.*
> *Watch out, oppressors. We are coming for you.*
> *Irhabioun anaa!!*

Fajjiroohum (Blow them up):
(Audio only)

> [0:30] *Blow them up... Blow them up where they stand and behead them and kick them out.*
> *And kick them out of the pure land...... and over whelm them with force.*

> [01:38] *Force them out and purify them.*
> *Get your justice.*
> *They are pigs and apes that spread disease on earth.*

> [02:10] *Destroy the Zionist and wipe them out*
> *No hudna [peace] or goodness in them*
> *Destroy those with no eib [shame]*

There are a many similar nasheeds on Islambase:[128]

Usud Al Harb (Lions of War)[129]
(Flash video with text)

> *In War we Are Lions, like eagles in the sky... We have inherited the cause*
> *We are knights, who have answered the call for war with our horses.*
> *Call us and we answer.*
> *For Allah we live and die, our aim to spread the message of Islam.*
> *For Allah to pass the message of Islam we answer the call of war.*
> *For God we fight and if we die we are the shuhuda.*
> *When war starts bullets mean nothing.*
>
> *We challenge death to defeat the enemy...*
> *Only for god we fight, and we ask him for victory as he is the one who created us.*

---

128 http://islambase.co.uk/index.php?option=com_content&task=category&sectionid=5&id=39&Itemid=183

129 http://islambase.co.uk/index.php?option=com_content&task=view&id=277&Itemid=183

If we die we have nothing to face but an eternity in heaven, it is not death as we will live forever.

Mother don't worry about me, my scars ...
If I die shaheed then rejoice, and if i return then rejoice as we are victorious as we love victory.

Labbayk Yaa Aqsa (Hail Aqsa)[130]
This is a reference to the al-Aqsa mosque in Jerusalem
(Flash video with text)

No! We will never forget and the time will come... no matter what happens or how long it takes.
We wash from zamzam [holy well in Mecca] and we will pray in al aqsa, hail aqsa, hail aqsa...
Our first kiblah [focus of prayer] for us, it is not easy for and with the group of friends the imam was our prophet.
But the day will come, o Muslims will rise, hail, the jihad has started.
No we will never forget...

Hayya Alal (Come on the Jihad)
(Flash video – footage of IDF oppression/Hamas)

The jihad is calling for you
We hate oppression, we are not cowards. In the path of allah... You cowards, it is our time to make war... It's time for revenge

Aseerun (Prisoners)[131]
(Video featuring still shots of prisoners in Guantanamo)

A caged prisoner in their prisons, they take our pride and our honour. They are tortured...
They have taken them from Pakistan to Cuba and tortured them.
You cowards it is time for revenge
Those who are listening to our message....
I will swipe them and spill their blood.... I will stay strong ...
Oh father I will remain in the sky, and return to the days of Salah Al Deen...

---

130 http://islambase.co.uk/index.php?option=com_content&task=view&id=278&Itemid=183

131 http://islambase.co.uk/index.php?option=com_content&task=view&id=121&Itemid=183

Al Quds Tonadeena (Al-Quds [Jerusalem] is calling out for us) by Ahmed Bukhatir[132]
(The video is linked to Youtube. It starts with the sound of machine guns and explosions and the video is stills of Palestinian fighters, general intifada imagery and Israeli army brutality)

> *Al Quds is calling out for us.*
> *The house of quds will return to our ummh and we will purify her court yard*
> *place above her our rayatuna (colours/flag)...*
> *Sons of Palestine be patient as god is making us close and the quds will return*
> *to us,*
> *To become once more our home and nation*

Many Islambase users admit liking pro-jihadist nasheeds. For example, on 16 February 2006, 'Umm Abdullah', a female user of Islambase posted a request "Can you please post some jihadi nasheeds". In response, 'Abu Sulayman' sent her a link to an external website with a selection of appropriate nasheeds.[133] Other requests have resulted in similar links being provided to a range of nasheeds supporting jihadist violence and al-Qaeda.[134]

---

132 http://islambase.co.uk/index.php?option=com_content&task=view&id=998&Itemid=183

133 http://forum.islambase.co.uk/index.php?showtopic=2521

134 http://forum.islambase.co.uk/index.php?showtopic=753

CHAPTER 5:

E-Conversations

In addition to distributing the recorded speeches and PDF documents, websites such as Islambase amongst others, also contain forums and blogs where readers can chat to each other. These online conversations illustrate the views of website users and demonstrate how they interpret and act on the extremist literature which they read and circulate. Many of the comments left on these areas of websites also glorify terrorist violence and imprisoned extremists. These forums play a key role in allowing extremists around the UK to meet and communicate with each other. In addition, the forums are important in creating online communities of like-minded individuals in which adhering to jihadist ideals may come to seem socially acceptable, theologically correct and, ultimately, an Islamic obligation. Furthermore they potentially allow young Muslims who stumble on websites like Islambase to come into direct contact with veterans of groups like al-Muhajiroun and other extremist organisations.

Recent terrorism trials have revealed how some individuals have been swiftly radicalised after taking part in online conversations on extremist internet forums. For example, Younis Tsouli, a Moroccan-born British citizen living in West London, began taking part in online discussions on radical forums in 2003. By 2004, he was stealing credit-cards details online and hacking into websites to transform them into al-Qaeda message-boards while creating websites for al-Qaeda's members in Iraq.[135] He then began distributing information on how to build car bombs and suicide bomb-vests while also communicating with terrorist cells in Scandinavia and the Balkans.[136] In December 2007, he was sentenced to 16 years in prison for offences under the 2006 Terrorism Act.[137]

---

135 *The Times:* 'Terrorist 007 'was internet propagandist for al-Qaeda". 26 April 2007. http://business.timesonline.co.uk/tol/business/law/article1706787.ece, The Washington Post: 'Terrorist 007, Exposed' (26 March 2007) http://www.washingtonpost.com/wp-dyn/content/article/2006/03/25/AR2006032500020.html

136 *The Telegraph:* '45 Muslim doctors planned US terror raids'. 6 July 2007. http://www.telegraph.co.uk/news/main.jhtml?xml=/news/2007/07/05/nterror405.xml

137 *BBC:* 'Longer sentences for al-Qaeda men'. 18 December 2007. http://news.bbc.co.uk/1/hi/uk/7150641.stm

Similarly, Sohail Qureshi, a British-born man of Pakistani origin, appeared to radicalise himself mainly through extremist websites before seeking to travel to Pakistan to aid the Taliban. Before leaving he wrote to friends on a Islamic forum: "I am not going for good as far as I know, it is only a 14 to 20 day operation, if it's in Pak, Afg or Waz."[138] He also posted a "farewell" letter, anonymously, on another website. He also contacted Samina Malik ('The Lyrical Terrorist') who ran a pro-terrorist blog and worked at Heathrow airport to ask about security procedures there before he attempted to fly to Pakistan with thousands of pounds in cash, terrorist training manuals and military night-vision equipment.[139]

On Jihad

Although Islambase users rarely directly call for jihadist attacks, many individuals who post on the website's forums discuss jihad in a positive manner and endorse the idea of the West being punished. They also frequently celebrate jihadist attacks on British troops.

For example, on 15 April 2008 'Hamza' posted a story from The Times about how a military inquest had heard that "six British soldiers serving in Iraq were killed by the same Western-made rifle within three months last year." One reader, 'Muslim_bro' responded to this news by writing "allahu akbar".[140]

In other cases, writers call for divine punishment to fall on the West. For example, on 7 February 2008, 'Abu Abdur-Rahman' responded to news that Abu Hamza would be extradited to the US to stand trial by writing:

"May Allah swt send his wrath upon the mujrimeen and destroy their nations by the hand of truth and deliver to them storms and hurricanes, calamity after

138 *The Daily Mail:* 'The dentist terrorist: British Muslim who planned to murder UK troops jailed' 8 January 2008. http://www.dailymail.co.uk/pages/live/articles/news/news.html?in_article_id=506841&in_page_id=1770

139 *BBC:* 'Man jailed over terrorism charges'. 8 January 2008. http://bl137w.blu137.mail.live.com/mail/InboxLight.aspx?FolderID=00000000-0000-0000-0000-0000000000001&InboxSortAscending=False&InboxSortBy=Date&n=1874843756

140 http://forum.islambase.co.uk/index.php?showtopic=3447&hl=akbar

calamity and tragedy followed by despair and grief. May Allah swt protect our dear brother and make for him jannah his final abode."[141]

In other cases, individuals seem to incite violence against Muslims who they believe have betrayed or abandoned Islam. On 20 December 2007, 'Dawud UK' wrote on Islambase that a Muslim British soldier whose face was shown on a TV programme should be "found" and "dealt with":

"My mrs called me in to watch one part of this were they showed a "muslim" soldier, during the scene a racist is told to work in a muslim shop in bradford (i think), but anyway if that shop can be found so can the friend of the shop-keeper who is the soldier and he can then be advised on his errors but the point it is he has put his face on national tv, his neighbourhood shouldnt be hard to find and therefore he can be found also inshallah and he can be cor-rected and dealt with."[142]

Some of the blogs popular with the users of Islambase similarly con-tain ambiguous messages which could be interpreted as incitement to terrorism. For example, on 13 January 2008 a blog entry appeared at the website unitedummah.wordpress.com entitled "Rise against op-pression". [143] The writer said that British Muslims who were not fully pre-occupied with the concerns of Muslims around the world were not being true to their faith:

"Britain continues to support Israeli (Jewish) and American aggression towards Muslims, bomb and kill Muslims in Iraq and Afghanistan, raid Muslim homes and arrest innocent Muslim men and women under bogus "anti-terror" laws. Yet despite all of this, people still have the audacity to say, "What oppression? I'm not being oppressed!" ... Moreover, they are not fulfilling their respon-sibilities (working to establish the Shari'ah, challenging falsehood and publicly exposing the evil in society), and that is why they cannot feel the oppression and tyranny of the Kuffaar, as the Prophet (SAW) and his Companions (RA) felt."

The entry's final phrase could be seen either as ambiguous or as a coded call for violence:

---

141 http://forum.islambase.co.uk/index.php?showtopic=2419

142 http://forum.islambase.co.uk/index.php?showtopic=2011

143 http://unitedummah.wordpress.com/2008/01/13/rise-against-oppression/

"Muslims should do what they have been ordered to do and leave the outcome to Allah (SWT)."

On the radicalisation of children

As many former members of groups like al-Muhajiroun grow older, get married and have children, so they increasingly become concerned with passing on their ideas to younger generations. Many posts on Islambase forums and on other websites popular with Islambase members reveal a deep pre-occupation with radicalising children.

For example, a British woman who runs the the unitedummah.wordpress.com blog often writes of how she aims to pass on her pro-jihadist ideas to her children. On one blog entry, entitled "Education – A Mother's Perspective' which dates from 1 December 2007, she writers:

> "As a Muslim woman and mother living in this kufr society, it is difficult for me to go by my day-to-day practises without being exposed to some kind of kufr. It's hard enough to refrain from looking at it, let alone explain to my two-and-a-half year old daughter that not everyone is a Muslim. Al-Hamdulillah though, she knows the difference between a kaafir and a Muslim. Some days she'll stand at the window telling me she's looking at the kaafir go by. Other days when I speak to her about Sheikh Usaamah, she'll think about it and reply with 'Go away kaafir', and raise her hand as if to hit someone ... How can we say 'Laa ilaaha illallaah' and allow our children to be educated (and dictated) by the kuffaar in school everyday? With the introduction in the last few years of Citizenship into the Curriculum, we are allowing our children to be taught that they must give allegiance to the Queen, and have hatred towards our great scholars and Mujaahideen. In English, as part of GCSE, they must study Shakespeare, whose books are full of homosexuality, fornication and adultery, each of which are great sins in Islam."[144]

Many of the Islambase forum's members seem similarly concerned with passing on their radical beliefs to their children. On 23 March 2008, 'Hamza' posted on Islambase a friend's account of how his son had replied when asked how he would respond if his father was killed by the "kuffar". The son told him:

> "You kaffirs didnt do anything to my dad. He wasn't afraid when you killed

---

144 http://unitedummah.wordpress.com/2008/01/12/education-a-mothers-perspective/

him. You only got him before he got you. It makes me really mad and I will take revenge on you and will never stop until you leave the Muslims alone! I will use all weapons on you cause you killed my dad and millions of Muslims. I will even die to protect Muslims if I go to jihad but if you kill my dad you better run cause I won't stop and Allah will protect me insha allah. I dont care if you kill me cause I'm not afraid of you or to die for Allah, and i'll have alot of wives in jennah insha allah and I'll be with my dad in jennah too and we will have fun doing what we want there if allah lets us. Don't kill my dad or you will be in trouble with me, I swear by Allah. Rashid bin Ali (9 years old)

"When Rashid read it to Usamah (my middle son), Usamah said 'Rashid I'll go with you too' with a smile on his face. Khattab (second to youngest) said, 'yeah and I will punch the kaffirs face'.

"Subhan allah, I had to leave the room and make sajood to Allah for giving me such good children who love allah so much and their dad. My kids never cease to amaze me. May Allah make them enter the army of Mehdi and Isa [Jesus], amen."[145]

One reader, 'Mujahidinbeeston', responded to the post by writing "Mashallah.... We could all learn something from the behaviour of children sometimes!! They sometimes say things so basic and plain, that when contemplated, makes so much sense!"[146]

In early 2008, these concerns were addressed directly by Omar Bakri in a talk entitled 'Upbringing' which was posted on the sawtulislam website on 12 April 2008.[147] He said:

"[07:35] I believe there is desperate need in this time and everywhere for da'i's [callers to Islam] whom are working day and night to produce new generations for the Muslim ummah with the correct belief and those da'i's are the parent and the fathers and the mothers and the brothers and the sisters are the teachers and everyone one of you are the frontier of the dawa of Islam, one of the frontier of this deen…or you are father or you are a person who work in any business of you are mujahid, you have a role to produce new generation to carry the correct aqeeda, have the correct minhaj (belief)."

145 http://forum.islambase.co.uk/index.php?showtopic=3002 – Nb. punctuation has been partially amended for ease of reading. The Mehdi is a figure in Islamic theology who will come to earth at the end of time in order to redeem humanity.

146 http://forum.islambase.co.uk/index.php?showtopic=3002

147 http://www.sawtulislam.com/?p=337

He adds that children should be brought up to become "capable" of spreading Islam either through dawa [missionary activity] or through jihad:

> "[22:21] When we are speaking about build the individuals we are talking about develop them and build them properly to become capable to carry the dawa and capable to carry the task whether in the dawa field or in the jihad battlefield."

The idea of radicalising children is given further support from theological texts distributed through other websites popular with Islambase users. For example, the tibyan.wordpress.com website hosts a PDF copy of the book '39 Ways to Serve and Participate in Jihad' by Muhammad bin Ahmad as-Salim (also known as 'Isa al-'Awshin) which contains a chapter 'Raise your children to love jihad and its people', in which as-Salim writes:

> "One's family and children are the preparation for the future and are themselves the future generation, so it is a must to raise one's family and children upon the love of jihad and the mujahidin, and the concepts of martyrdom and sacrifice for the Religion of Allah."[148]

On 3 May 2008, Islambase users discussed the possibility of adopting children and bringing them up.[149] A woman, 'Umm 3 Muslimahs', joined the discussion, writing "any ideas how you can actually get hold of an orphan? Also has anyone on here done it? [...] Any more info would be much appreciated".

'Abu Hamza al-Britani', one of the most prolific users of Islambase, also declared his interest in adopting, writing "i dont know about orphans but i am looking to foster a muslim child insha Allah in the very near future and would also like some info regrading this , if anyone can help us, or direct us towards where more info is available."

---

148 http://tibyan.wordpress.com/2007/08/24/39-ways-to-serve-and-participate-inji-had/ (nb. the PDF of this tibyan publication is stored at www.archive.org, a US-based website. The tibyan website provides a direct link to the article. The quote is from page 46 of the PDF.)

149 http://forum.islambase.co.uk/index.php?showtopic=3676&hl=adopt

On anti-terrorism measures

Users of websites like Islambase seem highly aware of how anti-terrorism laws may be used against them and take measures to prevent themselves being prosecuted.

On 20 June 2007, one Islambase user 'Islamic roast' posted extracts from the 2006 Terrorism Act onto the website's forum, writing that the legislation is "something i feel we as muslims are totally ignorent of, we need to be clued up with the laws of the kufar".[16] A lengthy discussion then followed with the site's users discussing past terrorism cases and how material downloaded from the internet can be considered evidence of supporting terrorism.

As a result of this and other discussions, Islambase users are very wary of being tricked by members of the security services into endorsing or encouraging acts of terrorism. For example, on 3 January 2008, 'death-aroundthecorner', a relatively inactive member of Islambase, asked readers of the forum whether it was permissible to carry out jihad in the absence of a caliphate:

> "All my life ive been brought up on the concept that there cannot be a jihad without a khalifate. but from listening to the lectures this does not seem to be the case. how can brothers do jihad there is no unity or organisation as such. i just need some clarifiacation its easy to say jihad is the answer but how???"

Regular Islambase readers reacted cautiously to the question, perhaps suspecting the writer to be a provocateur from the security services. One reader refers him to 'The Defence of Muslim Lands' by Abdullah Azzam. The forum's administrator replies, "£'m suprised [sic] the talks you've listened to did not give any clarification." 'Abu Abdur-Rahman' attempts to end the thread by writing:

> "Alhamdulilah if youve managed to grasp the understanding that there is jihad and it is an obligation from the talks then it seems youve benefited. Unfortunately thats as far as anyone on this forum can help you. If your looking at how to fight the jihad there are many different opinions presented by the mujahideen/terrorists whatever you may call them however as i said, none of us here fall into that category. You need to really watch them videos which pop up now again if you want to know what to do according to those who are actually fighting."

In another, later post, "Abu Abdur-Rahman" sarcastically tells the ques-

59

tioner to watch "Dispatches, Panorama etc" for information on how to join the jihad and then tells him that:

> "According to the information given by the kuffar in the previously mentioned programmes, here are the ways someone can get 'connected':
>
> 1/ attend extremist gatherings, talks or conferences held by al-muhajiroun/ saved sect/al-ghuraba etc..(they love associating anyone with these groups)
>
> 2/ visit extremist websites/forums that talk about jihad and how to do it.
>
> 3/ meet fellow jihadists online and form a sleeper cell
>
> 4/ travel to pakistan and visit a madrassa under the pretence of attending a mates wedding"[150]

Similarly, in a discussion about Omar Bakri on Islambase on 17 March 2008, the Islambase moderator joins the debate to point out that the website is not run by Omar Bakri:

> "The fact that we have Sheikh Omar's talks on Islambase does not mean we are ALM [al-Muhajiroun] rather we have much respect for the Sheikh, May Allah protect him from harm"[151]

In other cases, members freely mock anti-terror initiatives. For example, on 6 March 2008, 'Abu Hamza al-britani' wrote on the Islambase forum about government plans to introduce ID cards:

> "Alhamdu lillah [praise be to God], the world has failed to create an ID or travel document that us pakis have not been able to forge :-) it's not a matter of "can they?"... more of "when will they?"[152]

In a few instances forum members do feel secure enough to discuss jihad honestly – albeit still in a guarded fashion. On 4 March 2008, an online discussion began about a conference to be held by the Tayyibun Institute on the subject 'Reviving the Sunnah, Awakening the Ummah'. One user "Adil_11_1" joined the discussion saying:

---

150 http://forum.islambase.co.uk/index.php?showtopic=2114

151 http://forum.islambase.co.uk/index.php?showtopic=2898&hl=

152 http://forum.islambase.co.uk/index.php?showtopic=2755

"Correct me if im wrong but the only sunnah which i think is absent and needs to be revived today is the j ... i think that is what the ummah needs to focus on".

In this context "J" seems a clear reference to jihad. It is understood as such by "Abu Hamza al-Britani" who replies that "correction.... the j is not a sunnah its fard ayn" – a reference to the mainstream understanding that jihad is not part of the sunnah, i.e. the practices followed by Muhammad, but rather an Islamic duty revealed through the Quran.[153]

Similarly on 8 February 2008, a woman, 'Umm Sabah' writes that she is considering hijrah [emigration] to a country where "S-J aqeedah" (i.e. Salafi-Jihadi beliefs) are more accepted than in the UK:

"We're also still working on hijra. i was recommended as an option indonesia. because SJ aqeedah is left alone and allowed to be propogated and practiced openly....."[154]

---

153 http://forum.islambase.co.uk/index.php?showtopic=2736&st=0&p=14232&#entry 14232

154 http://forum.islambase.co.uk/index.php?showtopic=2102

CHAPTER 6

Distribution of leaflets

Several websites associated with Islambase contain leaflets, often in PDF form, which give extremist perspectives on issues such the hijab, halal meat and other matters relating to Muslims living in the UK.

For example, the Islambase.co.uk site contains leaflets on halal meat, telling readers that eating meat which is not halal may mean that the eater "will not enter paradise", that they will "incur the wrath of Allah" and that the act often "leads to apostacy".[155] The leaflet features the Islambase logo and web address. The leaflets relating to hijab says that Muslim women must cover everything apart from "the face and hands" and says that it should be worn "to differentiate the Muslimah [Muslim women] from the non-Muslims and the men".[156]

The content of these leaflets – which are credited to Islambase Productions – represent conservative Islamic positions. It is possible that putting the leaflets online are part of a wider strategy of making extremist publications accessible online to whoever needs them. Making the leaflets freely available online also allows the group's members to operate independently of each other, using the Islambase website as a virtual hub for their operations. Distribution of the leaflets on streets can also attract new readers to the Islambase website.

In some cases, users of the Islambase forum discuss the best ways to distribute such leaflets. For example, on 10 April 2008, 'Dawud UK', requested advice and feeback on some A5 leaflets about Islam which he had written:

> "We are doing some leafleting outside the local catholic church this saturday night before they have their mass, need some feedback on this leaflet below and another one below that."[157]

---

155 http://www.islambase.co.uk/publications/meatbw/

156 http://www.islambase.co.uk/publications/hijabbw/

157 http://forum.islambase.co.uk/index.php?showtopic=3348&st=0&#entry17282

One of the leaflet which he asked for feedback on was entitled 'The Trinity is blasphemy' and the other 'Jesus is a Muslim'.

The Islambase website also hosts PDFs of 'The Islamic Observer', a news-letter apparently published by al-Muhajiroun members. However only four issues are available and the most recent issue dates from December 2004.[158] Similarly, evidence that the leaflets are not regularly updated comes from a double-sided pamphlet on *shirk*, or idolatry, which is il-lustrated with a clearly dated picture of David Beckham wearing an England shirt.[159] The dated nature of the some of this material per-haps indicates how much damage has been done to radical groups since July 2005. In particular, the breaking up of radical networks based in mosques such as that at Finsbury Park and the strengthening of laws against incitement appear to have made it harder (and more risky) for extremists to produce leaflets and other material.

---

158 http://www.islambase.co.uk/downloads/iob/Dec04.pdf

159 http://www.islambase.co.uk/publications/shirk

CHAPTER 7:

Organisation of events

One of the roles of the Islambase website is to organise and publicise talks and lectures. In some cases, the events are mainstream and diverse. In other instances, however, the talks feature members of British radical Islamist circles. Examples of the advertised events include:

On 10 February, "GKT ISOC", a member claiming to represent the Guy's, King's & St. Thomas' Islamic Society advertised one of their upcoming lectures 'The path to protection…finding our way to Jannah' which would take place at the London Muslim Centre (LMC) on Islambase on 7th March 2008.[160] Although the event had a broad range of speakers, such as the US preacher Suhaib Webb and Sulayman Moola from South Africa, it also featured Riyadh ul-Haq, an extremist British Deobandi preacher. According to The Times, ul-Haq has previously given sermons praising martyrdom and saying that Muslims should "be willing to sacrifice anything that may be required of us" in order to liberate the al-Aqsa Mosque in Jerusalem[161]. In January 2008, the islamicnetwork.com website listed another talk by ul-Haq on the subject 'In The Footsteps of The Mother of The Believers', to be held on 24 February. The flyer for the event said "Shaykh Abu Yusuf Riyadh ul Haq will explore this topic from a unique angle, extracting morals and lessons from the lives of the noble wives of the Prophet Muhammad [pbuh]. These extracted morals and lessons will not be abstract, but will be applicable to the women of today (in this society)."[162]

On 8 February 2008, sawtulislam advertised a talk on the subject 'Shari'ah is the future for Britain' at which Anjem Choudary, formerly the deputy-leader of Omar Bakri's al-Muhajiroun, would be speaking. The talk was scheduled in response to the Archbishop of Canterbury's suggestion that aspects of the Sharia could be incorporated into the British legal system. A short essay advertising the event attacked both the

---

160 http://forum.islambase.co.uk/index.php?showtopic=2453

161 *The Times:* 'The homegrown cleric who loathes the British'. 7 September 2007. http://www.timesonline.co.uk/tol/news/uk/article2402998.ece

162 http://talk.islamicnetwork.com/showthread.php?t=14544

65

archbishop and other Muslims for suggesting that only parts of Sharia law could be implemented and said: "For any Muslim to even suggest that the Shari'ah should not be implemented in its entirety is an act of apostasy."[163]

British extremists also use Islambase and similar websites to trade ideas and suggestions about how to organise future events. For example, Islambase users have sought to arrange talks at university Islamic societies. On 11 March 2008, for example, "Abu Aisha" asked members of the Islambase forum if they could recommend speakers who could give a talk on marriage to London Metropolitan University's Islamic Society – adding that the university chaplain unfortunately no longer allowed preachers who were "hot" or "radical".[164] In response, several members suggested speakers. On another occasion, Islambase members discussed going to Speakers' Corner in London's Hyde Park to spread their views.[165] Some members argued that this could be a suitable venue for pro-jihadist talks. "Jameel" wrote: "I have been told that all the terrorism laws, glorifying terrorism etc dont apply there. So at speakers corner you actually get 'freedom of speech'". Further members suggested that consulting Omar Bakri to see what he suggested.[166]

163 http://www.sawtulislam.com/?p=202

164 http://forum.islambase.co.uk/index.php?showtopic=2804

165 http://forum.islambase.co.uk/index.php?showtopic=734&mode=linear

166 See section on Omar Bakri in Chapter 1.

CHAPTER 8:

Messages from prisoners

One of the most important roles of radical websites is to distribute communications from individuals imprisoned on terrorism-related charges.
In many cases, imprisonment seems to have enhanced their reputation
amongst users of Islambase and other similar websites.

One of the most notable prisoners to pass communications from prison
is Dhiren Barot (known on the websites as Issa Barot). Barot, a Hindu-
born convert who attended militant training camps in Pakistan in the
mid-1990s, was convicted in November 2006 after pleading guilty of
conspiracy to murder.[167] He was found guilty of planning to carry out
bombing attacks in London and the US. On 28 November 2007, cap-
tivesupport.org posted a lengthy letter from Barot describing his expe-
riences in prison. Although captivesupport was not listed by Islambase
users as one of their favourite websites, it is frequently mentioned in
online discussions. Barot's letter details incidents of abuse and violence
which he said he had suffered from both fellow prisoners and prison
officials during his time in jail. He also calls for Muslims to offer more
"support" to imprisoned extremists and mocks the "biryani and coca-
cola existence" of ordinary British Muslims. The letter contains no overt
calls for violence.[168]

The same website contains three poems by a man described as "Abu
Sumayyah – Held Hostage at a UK Prison." Elsewhere on the website,
the name 'Abu Sumayyah' is explained as the pseudonym of Mizanur
Rahman.[169] Rahman was convicted in November 2006 of "stirring up
racial hatred" during a demonstration outside the Danish embassy in
London earlier that year.[170] During the protest he called for further "9-
11" attacks and held up a placard which said: "Annihilate those who

---

167 *BBC:* 'Al-Qaeda plotter jailed for life'. 7 November 2006. http://news.bbc.co.uk/1/
hi/uk/6123236.stm

168 http://www.captivesupport.org/?p=50

169 http://www.captivesupport.org/?p=10

170 *BBC:* 'Cartoons protestor found guilty'. 9 November 2006. http://news.bbc.co.uk/1/
hi/uk/6133516.stm

insult Islam." Abu Sumayyah poems, all apparently written in prison, are largely metaphorical reflections on global politics. For example, one poem compares the US to a person who attacks a beehive and then asks:

"Why did all these Bumblebees,
Suddenly start stinging me?
They must be angry terrorists
Jealous of my freedom!"[171]

The site also features a poem by Abdul Rahman Saleem, a former al-Muhajiroun spokesman, who was also sentenced to four years in prison for his part in the Danish embassy demonstration[172]. His poem begins by defending his role in the demonstration:

"For the honour of Muhammad (saw) I was demonstrating,
In London's streets "Laa ilaaha illallah Muhammadur Rasoolullah" I was reciting,
Hands off Habibullah and we love Rasoolullah I was repeating,
And Islam is superior and can never be surpassed I was chanting." [173]

It ends by calling on British Muslims to continue struggling against non-Muslims until Islam dominates the world:

"But for now I remind you my dear brothers and sisters to never stop calling,
And let the Lions of Islam in the East and West keep on roaring, against tyranny and dictatorship you must continue struggling,
Because with every call and every roar the walls and pillars of kufr and shirk keep on crumbling.
And there is no doubt day by day, hour by hour and minute by minute this deen keeps on rising,
For verily a day will come where in every corner of this globe and in every nation the black and white flag of Islam will be flying,
And like a cool breeze, justice, tranquillity and prosperity for Muslims and non-Muslims alike will indeed be spreading."

The website also contains a letter which was written in prison by Rajib Khan who was tried alongside Abu Izzadeen in early 2008 on charges

171 http://www.captivesupport.org/?p=104

172 *BBC:* 'The angry young men jailed over protest'. 18 July 2007. http://news.bbc.co.uk/1/hi/uk/6903445.stm

173 http://www.captivesupport.org/?p=111

of funding terrorism.[174] The letter compares the trials of prison life with the future delights of paradise:

> "Even though we were taken to prison in handcuffs and wear the prison clothes and eat the prison food, Insha-Allah if we are successful and be from those that Allah (swt) is pleased with, then we shall be adorned with bracelets of gold, wear the clothes of Jannah – green silk robes with embroidery of gold, we shall eat from the utensils of gold and silver."[175]

Khan was acquitted of all charges, including inciting terrorism overseas on 18 April 2006. He was found not guilty of funding-raising for terrorists and the jury was unable to reach a decision on charges of inciting terrorism overseas.[176] He was told that he would not face a re-trial.[177] Despite this, his letter remains on the captivesupport website.

In addition the website contains a letter from Omar Abdel Rahman who is in prison in the US for his role in the 1993 World Trade Centre bombing.[178] The letter recounts his trials in prisons and calls for Muslims around the world to rise up:

> "O people of sacrifice and dignity. O men of Allah! Rise up from your deep slumber. Rise up with your resounding voices. Set out, O men of Allah, and let your voices be heard in every place, and say it with all your strength and loudly, without fear. Rise up, O men of Allah and like one body, show the truth and negate the evil. 'And don't give in to those who aggress, lest the fire take hold of you.'"

In addition to distributing messages from prisoners, the Islambase website also co-ordinates the sending of material to prisoners. For example, on 18 November 2007, 'abudujana 2006' wrote on the Islambase forum:

---

174 *BBC:* 'Six men charged under terror act'. 29 April 2007. http://news.bbc.co.uk/1/hi/uk/6606227.stm

175 http://www.captivesupport.org/?p=30

176 Crown Prosecution Service. Press release: 'Six men sentenced over terrorism charges'. 18 April 2008. http://www.cps.gov.uk/news/pressreleases/127_08.html

177 *The Yorkshire Post:* 'Terror accused walk free'. 28 April 2008. http://www.yorkshire-post.co.uk/news/Terror-accused-walk-free.4023630.jp

178 http://www.captivesupport.org/?p=54

"i was wondering if anyone has any notes on topics such as tawakkul,reliance ,hope,fear,love etc...in details with their definitions,classifications etc. also any articles on trials and tribulations would much be appreciated. it is for a brother behind bars."[179]

The same day, 'UmmWala', a female members of Islambase, responded, writing:

"How soon are the notes needed? I have most of them i think but i need to look for them. Also Sheikh [possibly referring to Omar Bakri] did a nice topic on Tawakkul wa Sabr yesterday but the notes need to be edit[ed]."

---

179   http://forum.islambase.co.uk/index.php?showtopic=1793]

CHAPTER 9:

Who uses these websites?

It is not easy to estimate how many people read Islambase and similar website. In 11 April, a typical day, a visitor-counter on the Islambase forum recorded 581 registered members and said that 47 members had been on the forums that day. The website also records how many times each post on the forums are read. Some popular posts are read as many as 1,500 times; the least popular record only one or two readers – the average seems to be around 60-70 readers per post. The sawtulislam website forum claims similar levels of membership, recording 291 registered members. Most other websites popular with Islambase users do not reveal their user statistics.

Members of the Islambase forum have discussed ways to bring new readers onto the website. On 2 January 2008, 'Dawud UK' wrote:

"This forum and especially the website seem extremely good mashallah, but how do we boost numbers? as i tend to get kicked off or leave most other forums so i cant spread the word myself (had three different id's blocked on the ahle haddith forum islamicboard.com since i started kussing the saudi salafi scholars) but only thing i can suggest is we get personal contacts and those who seem close to the truth on other boards on here."[180]

A woman, 'Umm Abdullah', replied:

"We defo [definitely] need more people here because it will make us more confident forbidding the munkar [evil] and enjoining the good as we'll here about more people doing it, and it will encourage us to keep doing what we do and create more ideas inshallah. I'll let the sisters I know to come and join the forum, there doesnt seem to be many sisters on this board come to think of it."

Another woman, 'Umm Sabah', added:

"These days good forums tend to be quite inactive, while the more liberal ones are thriving… which is sad. there are rare gems where the forum is v[ery] nice and the members are active and beneficial."

---

180 http://forum.islambase.co.uk/index.php?showtopic=2102

Similarly, on 26 March 2008, 'Abu Aisha' wrote that on an Islambase forum that:

> "I thought it might be a nice idea if all the members on the forum got together and posted up really really useful material for tarbiya purposes [i.e. educational] for non-Muslims and Jaahil [ignorant] brothers and sisters."[181]

He further suggested that tafseers (interpretations of the Quran), biographies and hadith collections could be posted online to help bring in more readers.

---

181 http://forum.islambase.co.uk/index.php?showtopic=3058

Summary: Extremist websites and radicalisation

Studying websites popular with Islambase users has given insights into how Islamic extremists do (and do not) use the internet:

Functions of extremist websites

❖ Online libraries

Extremist websites such as Islambase play a key role in storing and distributing radical texts teaching violent interpretations of Islam. Many of these justify violent jihad against non-Muslims and seek to legitimise the killing of Muslims who 'leave' Islam. Such websites also play a key role in distributing hard-to-find English translations of Arabic jihadist texts.

❖ Venue for preachers

Radical websites can act as online substitutes for physical locations such as Abu Hamza's former base in Finsbury Park mosque. On such websites, sermons by radical preachers (including those imprisoned for terrorism offences or inciting violence) can be listened to and one can meet and communicate with like-minded individuals on the forums.

❖ Organisational hub

Websites such as Islambase act as organisational hubs where extremists can plan, organise and discuss their activities around the UK. Leaflets stored and exchanged online in PDF form also allow extremists nationwide to co-ordinate their message on key issues.

What the websites don't do

❖ 'Virtual training camp'

Media reports of extremist websites such as Islambase being 'virtual training camps' are exaggerated. This study found no evidence of these websites of-

73

fering advice on bomb manufacturing, or on attending training camps abroad. However, once readers are convinced of the legitimacy of jihadist violence, instructions on creating bombs and explosives can be easily found elsewhere online.

❖ Indoctrinating casual visitors to websites

Reports of extremists setting up websites to 'radicalise' random individuals who stumble upon them appear largely unfounded. In most cases, radical websites seem to mainly cater to those who are already known in radical circles – as is evidenced by the password-protected nature of many such sites.

What the websites say about extremist networks in the UK

While websites such as Islambase reveal a great deal about how British extremists use the internet, they also indicate emerging trends in British jihadist networks as a whole. In many cases, however, such evidence is contradictory; sometimes evidence suggests that radical groups are becoming weaker, at other times, it appears that radical groups and ideologies are merely evolving in response to the UK's new anti-terrorism laws and wider developments affecting jihadist groups worldwide.

Evidence of extremist networks becoming weaker

❖ Shortage of pro-jihadist theologians in UK

Islambase users frequently complain about the lack of clerics in the UK who will provide theological justifications for jihadist attacks and takfiri ideology. They also complain that their present leaders – such as Anjem Choudary – lack the necessary theological training and knowledge of Arabic and cannot replace jailed clerics such as Abu Qatada.

❖ Effects of 2006 Terrorism Act

Laws prohibiting the 'glorification of terrorism' have led to radical speakers 'toning down' their public talks. Likewise, many comments left on online forums make frequent reference to the need to avoid falling foul of anti-terrorism laws. Younger radical speakers are also far more reluctant to openly incite violence than the previous generation of radical clerics such as Abu Hamza, Abdullah Faisal and Abu Qatada.

74

❖ **Estrangement from Muslim community**

Individuals who use websites such as Islambase often admit to feeling para-noid and persecuted. While they often say they feel increasingly under attack from the government (paranoid references to being bugged by MI5 abound), they also admit to feeling shunned and rejected by the mainstream Muslim community.

❖ **Increasing dissent within extremist circles**

Online conversations between radicals show a wide divergence of theological views. Online discussion forums on websites such as Islambase frequently fea-ture increasingly heated debates over whether Omar Bakri is qualified scholar (many believe that he is not) and about the 'covenant of protection' which many believe exists between the British government and Muslims in the UK.

Evidence for the evolution of radical networks

❖ **Changing preaching style**

Preachers currently popular with UK extremists rarely openly advocate or defend jihadist attacks whether in the UK or abroad. Instead their style of rhetoric has become more allusive, for example, delivering lectures on how historical figures such as Salahuddin fought and defeated the Crusaders and encouraging Muslims emulate them and replicate their actions. This enables preachers to avoid overtly 'glorifying' terrorism while continuing to promote violence and hostility towards non-Muslims.

❖ **Growing localism**

In the 1990s, Islamic extremists operated openly in central London locations, such as Speakers Corner, and inside prominent mosques in Finsbury Park and Brixton. Today, users of extremist websites frequently refer to towns such as Luton and Leicester as being the centres of their operations, along with the Glyndon Community Centre in South-East London.

❖ **Increasing importance of private study circles**

One consequence of extremists shifting their operations away from high-pro-file mosques is that they place increasingly emphasis on attending private study circles and holding meetings in each other's homes (and even in restaurants and community centres). This development may make it increasingly difficult for the security services to monitor extremist networks and teachings.

❖ Incitement by extremists abroad

Islambase users regularly distribute communications and recorded lectures between extremists abroad and their UK-based followers. In particular, they circulate messages and talks from Omar Bakri in Lebanon and Abdullah Faisal in Jamaica. This shows that even if the government deports or exiles UK-based extremists, they can continue inciting their British followers from abroad.

❖ Emphasis on radicalising children

As former members of groups like al-Muhajiroun grow older, marry and have children, many increasingly discuss how to pass on their extremist interpretations of Islam to their children. Islambase users often discuss withdrawing their children from non-Muslim schools, teaching them radical Islamic ideas (through home-schooling and after-school classes) and training them to love martyrdom and to hate non-Muslims.

Conclusion

In the last few years, and particularly since 2005, the government and the security services have inflicted considerable damage to extremist Islamic networks in the UK. Radical preachers have been jailed or deported. Overt recruitment on campuses and mosques has been largely curtailed. Channels for raising funds and communicating with jihadists abroad have been badly disrupted. However, one side-effect of this is that surviving Islamic extremists have shifted their activities onto the web. The government has in turn responded to this development by passing laws against glorifying terrorism which specifically aim to limit extremists' use of the internet.

Unfortunately, as this report shows, there is mounting evidence that the government's present approach to tackling online radicalisation is not fully succeeding and that laws against glorifying or promoting terrorism on the internet are not being adequately enforced. British-based extremists have established several websites which operate as centres of online radicalisation where texts advocating violent jihad, al-Qaeda videos glorifying terrorist violence and lectures by British extremists which overtly incite hatred are openly distributed. Underscoring the failure of the government's present strategy is that radical sermons by many individuals jailed for incitement to violence remain freely available online on websites run by their British followers. If the same individuals who run and use Islambase were distributing recorded lectures by Abu Hamza and Omar Bakri free of charge on street corners, they would be arrested and probably charged. But because they do so online they have not been prosecuted and as a result they continue to operate with impunity.

The government needs to continue pressuring radical groups wherever they exist in order to deny them freedom to recruit. In the fight against extremism, as in conventional war, governments should not give their enemy the chance to re-group and re-organise. Those who promote terrorism through the internet should be made to know that they will be held accountable.

Recommendations

It is important that pro-terrorist groups and individuals are not allowed to use the internet to spread their ideas and to recruit new followers. There are two separate routes that the government can take to limit extremist use of the internet:

Legal measures

❖ Prosecute individuals who run extremist websites or distribute pro-terrorism materials through them. The 2006 Terrorism Act specifically enables the prosecution of those who distribute material which glorifies terrorism attacks or is likely to encourage readers to undertake such actions.

❖ Prosecute Internet Services Providers (ISPs). Under the 2006 Terrorism Act, ISPs and other commercial organisations can be held liable for hosting websites whose content promotes terrorism. Some ISPs – like BT Group – already use a web filter called Cleanfeed in order to block websites which host unacceptable images of child pornography or sexual abuse.

❖ Explore whether laws used to tackle internet use by paedophiles can be adapted to tackle terrorism. For example, laws to tackle paedophilia allow prosecution of those who distribute and possess paedophilic images. They also criminalise online 'grooming' of children. Individuals found guilty can be banned from using the internet.

❖ Block foreign-based websites. In extreme cases, the government can ask UK-based Internet Service Providers (ISP) block foreign websites. Some European governments have already considered similar steps.[182]

---

182 For example, in 2002 the German state of North Rhine-Westphalia ordered 85 ISPs to block two foreign websites which incited racist violence. Source: Privacy International: 'Silenced: Censorship and Control of the Internet' Published 10 September 2003. Similarly, in September 2007, Franco Frattini, the European Commissioner for Justice, Freedom and Security said the EU should consider forcing European ISPs to block websites which give information on building bombs or which "are aimed at inspiring criminal activity". *The Daily Telegraph:* 'DIY bomb websites to be banned by Brussels'. 4 July 2007.

Such steps should only be taken against the most extreme websites and individuals because their widespread implementation would risk considerable – and perhaps unacceptable – curbs being placed on freedom of expression. These measures would also risk confirming the arguments made by many British Muslim extremists that the government is conspiring against Muslims and that anti-terror laws are applied disproportionately against Muslims (for instance, they could validly point out that government has not blocked neo-Nazi or far-right websites which advocate violence).

Engagement

If the government is unable to prosecute those who run extremist websites or is unable to block websites based abroad, other steps should be taken to challenge and undermine the messages and teachings put out by extremist websites. This could be done in several ways:

❖ British extremists who use radical online forums can be gradually engaged and challenged by government-sponsored web-users. Through taking part – covertly – in such online discussions, government users can question the extremists' assumptions, direct them to more moderate websites and challenge their interpretations of Islam.

❖ When extremists advertise upcoming events and talks online, the government could assist and encourage Muslim groups opposed to terrorism to attend the events in order to question radical speakers, promote moderation and challenge pro-jihadist interpretations of Islam and of current affairs.

❖ The government should also explore ways to promote more tolerant understandings of Islam through the internet. Financial support can be provided to moderate Islamic groups to expand their internet operations. One of the most popular features of Islambase is its online forum. UK-based Islamic extremists enjoy discussion and debate about Islam – the government should find a way to use this to promote moderation rather than greater radicalism.

Such non-confrontational approaches would also suit counter-terrorism officers who argue that extremist, pro-terrorism websites should be allowed to remain active because they provide important opportunities for the security services to monitor radical groups.

Any government action should initially be directed primarily against five websites which are the main online hubs for British extremist networks. These are:

- ❖ **islambase.co.uk**

- ❖ **sawtulislam.com**

- ❖ **kalamullah.com**

- ❖ **salafiyyah-jadeedah.tripod.com**

- ❖ **tibyan.wordpress**

Islambase discussion of favourite websites

On 29 October 2007, users of Islambase* had an online discussion about their favourite Islamic websites. This information has been used as the basis of this report.

---

* http://forum.islambase.co.uk/index.php?showtopic=1668&hl=favourite+websites

> Islambase Forum > General Forums > Discussions

Reply to this topicStart new topic

> Favourite Websites?

Options ∨

Hamza

post Oct 29 2007, 08:16 AM

Post #1

Advanced Member
***

Group: Brothers Moderators
Posts: 2,356
Joined: 16-June 07
From: I am where i am and i be where i be...
Member No.: 391
Gender: Muslim Male

Line them up people!

Its good to share. Im talking Islamic websites and things to do with the Deen like newsites etc where you can get good reliable info.

Please people dont find some artical on any site burried deep deep down somewhere and accuse the person of being a yusuf qardawi lover. It would be different if the person linked up www.iloveyusufqardawi.com or worse asktheimam.com!

Il list a few and InshAllah post a few more later.

http://moderatesrefuted.wordpress.com/

http://www.missionislam.com/knowledge/shia.htm

http://www.islamlecture.com/

http://www.islamawareness.net/Converts/

http://www.drkhalid.co.uk/

http://salafiyyah-jadeedah.tripod.com/

http://www.makedua.com/

http://www.kr-hcy.com/index2.shtml

http://www.ibnulqayyim.com/

http://www.islaam.com/

http://www.islam-qa.com/index.php?ln=eng

http://www.islaam.net/main/

http://tibyan.wordpress.com/

Abu Sa'id Al-Khudri reportedThat the Messenger of Allah (PBUH) said, "How can I feel at ease when the Angel of the Trumpet, (Israfil) has put his lips to the Trumpet and is waiting for the order to blow it".
[At-Tirmidhi]

"Allah has sent down the most beautiful of speech, a Book, (parts of it) resembling (others), often repeated. The skins of those who fear their Lord shiver from it. Then their skins and their hearts soften to

84

"Allah has sent down the most beautiful of speech, a Book, (parts of it) resembling (others), often repeated. The skins of those who fear their Lord shiver from it. Then their skins and their hearts soften to the remembrance of Allah." [Qur'an 39:23]

"Has not the time come for the hearts of those who believe to be affected by Allah's Reminder and that which has been revealed of the truth, lest they become as those who received the Scripture before, and the term was prolonged for them and so their hearts were hardened? And many of them were rebellious, disobedient (faasiqoon)." [Al-Hadeed, (57):16]

The Honour is upon the harsh backs of the Stallions, And glory is born from the wombs of sleepless nights & nocturnal journeys...

"The more I scream they will laugh and do it again... my screams all in vain."
Guant¹namo detainee Omar Deghayes

http://muslimprisonersupport.com/blog/

Go to the top of the pageReport Post | +Quote Post

---

abu aisha | post Oct 29 2007, 09:40 AM | Post #2

Advanced Member
**

Group: Brothers
Posts: 177
Joined: 13-April 07
Member No.: 138
Gender: Muslim Male

www.islambase.co.uk OBVIOUSLY
ders also:
www.kalamullah.com
www.islamicnetwork.com
www.sawtulislam.com
unitedummah.wordpress.com
faswj.wordpress.com
duaat.wordpress.com
captivesuk.wordpress.com
www.obmonline.net
www.mituk.org

Forum - 1dawah.ipbfree.com 1dawah.wordpress.com - **Blog**

1Dawah - www.1dawah.co.uk

Go to the top of the pageReport Post | +Quote Post

Hamza | post Oct 29 2007, 12:08 PM | Post #3

Advanced Member
**

Group: Brothers Moderators
Posts: 2,356
Joined: 16-June 07
From: I am where i am and i be where i e...
Member No.: 391
Gender: Muslim Male

SubhanAllah how could i forget www.kalamullah.com??

The amount of dua i make for the admin of that site!!

Abu Sa`id Al-Khudri reportedThat the Messenger of Allah (PBUH) said, "How can I feel at ease when the Angel of the Trumpet, (Israfil) has put his lips to the Trumpet and is waiting for the order to blow it". [At-Tirmidhi]

"Allah has sent down the most beautiful of speech, a Book, (parts of it) resembling (others), often repeated. The skins of those who fear their Lord shiver from it. Then their skins and their hearts soften to the remembrance of Allah." [Qur'an 39:23]

85

"Allah has sent down the most beautiful of speech, a Book, (parts of it) resembling (others), often repeated. The skins of those who fear their Lord shiver from it. Then their skins and their hearts soften to the remembrance of Allah." [Qur'an 39:23]

"Has not the time come for the hearts of those who believe to be affected by Allah's Reminder and that which has been revealed of the truth, lest they become as those who received the Scripture before, and the term was prolonged for them and so their hearts were hardened? And many of them were rebellious, disobedient (faasiqoon)." [Al-Hadeed, (57):16]

The Honour is upon the harsh backs of the Stallions, And glory is born from the wombs of sleepless nights & nocturnal journeys...

"The more I scream they will laugh and do it again... my screams all in vain."
Guantanamo detainee Omar Deghayes

http://muslimprisonersupport.com/blog/

Go to the top of the pageReport Post   +Quote Post

Abu Abdul-salaam   post Oct 29 2007, 05:40 PM   Post #4

Newbie
*

Group: Brothers
Posts: 7
Joined: 6-May 07
From: Ardullah
Member No.: 243
Gender: Muslim Male

> QUOTE
>
> http://obmonline.com - Website dedicated to Sheikh Omar Bakri Muhammad
>
> http://sawtulislam.com - Site and blog commited to presenting Islamic literature
>
> http://mituk.org - Muslims in the UK - presenting information to non-muslims providing real solutions to political and social problems in Britain.
>
> http://captivesuk.wordpress.com - Muslim Captives Support - Supporting the Muslim captives wherever they are.
>
> http://universityofyusuf.wordpress.com - Blog dedicated to the students from the University of Yusuf [as] (ie, the aseer).
>
> http://unitedummah.wordpress.com - Islamic blog presenting islamic literature - with islamic gallery.
>
> http://duaat.wordpress.com - Various topics highlighted on this blog, with details to a Live Paltalk room.

Abu Isa

Go to the top of the pageReport Post   +Quote Post

Hamza   post Oct 30 2007, 01:58 AM   Post #

Advanced Member
***

Group: Brothers Moderators
Posts: 2,356
Joined: 16-June 07
From: I am where i am and i be where i be...
Member No.: 391
Gender: Muslim Male

http://www.islamicthinkers.com/index/index.php

http://www.khutbah.com/

http://muslimconverts.com/

http://www.mysisterskeeper.com/articles.html

http://www.thepathtoparadise.com/

http://www.islamawareness.net/Jinn/

http://muttaqun.com/jinn.html

Quran and Hadith

http://www.thepathtoparadise.com/

http://www.mounthira.com/

http://www.transliteration.org/quran/home.htm

http://www.witness-pioneer.org/vil/hadeeth/riyad/

http://www.searchtruth.com/list.php

http://qtafsir.com/

http://ibnkathir.atspace.com/ibnkathir/

http://www.tafsir.com/

http://www.islamicity.com/mosque/SURAI.HTM

http://www.usc.edu/dept/MSA/reference/searchhadith.html

Abu Sa`id Al-Khudri reportedThat the Messenger of Allah (PBUH) said, "How can I feel at ease when the Angel of the Trumpet, (Israfil) has put his lips to the Trumpet and is waiting for the order to blow it". [At-Tirmidhi]

"Allah has sent down the most beautiful of speech, a Book, (parts of it) resembling (others), often repeated. The skins of those who fear their Lord shiver from it. Then their skins and their hearts soften to the remembrance of Allah." [Qur'an 39:23]

"Has not the time come for the hearts of those who believe to be affected by Allah's Reminder and that which has been revealed of the truth, lest they become as those who received the Scripture before, and the term was prolonged for them and so their hearts were hardened? And many of them were rebellious, disobedient (faasiqoon)." [Al-Hadeed, (57):16]

The Honour is upon the harsh backs of the Stallions, And glory is born from the wombs of sleepless nights & nocturnal journeys...

"The more I scream they will laugh and do it again... my screams all in vain."
Guantⁱ-namo detainee Omar Deghayes

http://muslimprisonersupport.com/blog/

~musaafira~

Newbie
*

Group: Sisters
Posts: 6
Joined: 26-July 07
From: taking shade under a tree
Member No.: 699
Gender: Muslimah Female

post Nov 1 2007, 06:28 PM

Post #

Jazakallahu khairun for the links

does anyone know what happened to caravanofmartyrs at wordpress sad.gif

Go to the top of the pageReport Post

+Quote Pos

---

abu aisha

Advanced Member
***

Group: Brothers
Posts: 177
Joined: 13-April 07
Member No.: 138
Gender: Muslim Male

post Nov 1 2007, 10:19 PM

Post #

> QUOTE(~musaafira~ @ Nov 1 2007, 02:28 PM) *
>
> Jazakallahu khairun for the links
>
> does anyone know what happened to caravanofmartyrs at wordpress sad.gif

and streetdawah

Forum - 1dawah.ipbfree.com 1dawah.wordpress.com - **Blog**
1Dawah - www.1dawah.co.uk

Go to the top of the pageReport Post

+Quote Pos

---

abdulrahman al m...

Advanced Member
***

Group: Brothers
Posts: 470
Joined: 21-March 07
Member No.: 46
Gender: Muslim Male

post Nov 2 2007, 09:40 PM

Post #

Bring back The saved sect and Ghuraba websites.

Clearly the best sites on the web

"What can my enemeies do to me? I have in my breast both my heaven and my garden. If I travel they are with me, never leaving me. Imprisonment for me is a chance to be with my Lord. To be killed is martyrdom & to be exiled from my land is a spiritual journey."

Go to the top of the pageReport Post

+Quote Pos

Hamza

Advanced Member
***

Group: Brothers Moderators
Posts: 2,356
Joined: 16-June 07

post Nov 2 2007, 09:51 PM

Post #

I sense a bit of a theme here.

Advanced Member
**

Group: Brothers Moderators
Posts: 2,356
Joined: 16-June 07
From: I am where i am and i be where i
be...
Member No.: 391
Gender: Muslim Male

I sense a bit of a theme here.

Abu Sa`id Al-Khudri reportedThat the Messenger of Allah (PBUH) said, "How can I feel at ease when the Angel of the Trumpet, (Israfil) has put his lips to the Trumpet and is waiting for the order to blow it". [At-Tirmidhi]

"Allah has sent down the most beautiful of speech, a Book, (parts of it) resembling (others), often repeated. The skins of those who fear their Lord shiver from it. Then their skins and their hearts soften to the remembrance of Allah." [Qur'an 39:23]

"Has not the time come for the hearts of those who believe to be affected by Allah's Reminder and that which has been revealed of the truth, lest they become as those who received the Scripture before, and the term was prolonged for them and so their hearts were hardened? And many of them were rebellious, disobedient (faasiqoon)." [Al-Hadeed, (57):16]

The Honour is upon the harsh backs of the Stallions, And glory is born from the wombs of sleepless nights & nocturnal journeys...

**"The more I scream they will laugh and do it again... my screams all in vain."
Guantánamo detainee Omar Deghayes**

http://muslimprisonersupport.com/blog/

Go to the top of the pageReport Post   +Quote Post

Enter Keywords   Search Topic   « Next Oldest · **Discussions** · Next Newest »

Fast ReplyReply to this topicStart new topic

User(s) are reading this topic (0 Guests and 0 Anonymous Users)

Members: aymanzahhar

▶ **Similar Topics**   **Collapse**

	Topic	Replies	Topic Starter	Views	Last Action
Hot Topic	Pinned: Favourite Books	40	abu aisha	526	16th April 2008 - 02:01 AM Last post by: Jameel
Hot Topic	Pinned: Favourite Speaker?	59	Hamza	578	13th April 2008 - 03:22 AM Last post by: abu hamza al-Britani
Closed	Favourite Super Hero Who's yours and why?	96	abu hamza al-Britani	538	19th March 2008 - 06:40 PM Last post by: Hamza

|-- Discussions   ▾ | Go |

English ▾   **Lo-Fi Version**   Time is now: 21st April 2008 - 04:22 PM

List of websites cited by Islambase users

http://moderatesrefuted.wordpress.com/

http://www.missionislam.com/knowledge/shia.htm

http://www.islamlecture.com/

http://www.islamawareness.net/Converts/

http://www.drkhalid.co.uk/

http://salafiyyah-jadeedah.tripod.com/

http://www.makedua.com/

http://www.kr-hcy.com/index2.shtml

http://www.ibnulqayyim.com/

http://www.islaam.com/

http://www.islam-qa.com/index.php?ln=eng

http://www.islaam.net/main/

http://tibyan.wordpress.com/

http://www.islambase.co.uk/

http://www.kalamullah.com/

http://www.islamicnetwork.com/

http://www.sawtulislam.com/

http://unitedummah.wordpress.com/

http://faswj.wordpress.com/

http://duaat.wordpress.com/

http://captivesuk.wordpress.com/

http://www.obmonline.net/

http://www.mituk.org/

http://universityofyusuf.wordpress.com/
http://islamicthinkers.com/index/index.php
http://www.khutbah.com/
http://muslimconverts.com/
http://www.mysisterskeeper.com/articles.html
http://www.pathtoparadise.com/
http://www.islamawareness.net/Jinn/
http://www.muttaqun.com/jinn.html
http://www.mounthira.com/
http://www.transliteration.org/quran/home.htm
http://www.witness-pioneer.org/vil/hadeeth/riyad/
http://www.searchtruth.com/list.php
http://qtafsir.com/
http://ibnkathir.atspace.com/ibnkathir/
http://www.tafsir.com/
http://www.islamicity.com/mosque/SURAI.HTM
http://www.usc.edu/dept/MSA/reference/searchhadith.html
http://ghurabaanews.blogspot.com/

Abu Bashir al-Tartusi on 'The covenant of security in Islam'

The following extract comes from a recorded lecture by Abu Bashir al-Tartusi, a Syrian wahhabi cleric, on 'The covenant of security' between the UK and its Muslim inhabitants. Speaking in Arabic – but followed by an English translation – he tells his audience that it is haram for Muslims legally resident in the UK to carry out jihadist attacks within Britain:

"[28:55] The prophet says that if a Muslim speaks, he speaks the truth and if he gives his trust, he never betrays his trust; and if he gives his trust of security, he'll never betray that … [29:50] We wanted to confirm how the prophet was very specific that we must not betray our trust so we can learn how. We want to re-affirm how we must not betray our trust and how he's made it so severe and haram and prohibited to betray your trust. This is not a matter of one and two texts and that's it – there are tens and tens of texts speaking about this matter. This should always make us stop and limit ourselves only the limits of Allah subhan Allah and restrict ourselves to that only. We've mentioned the hadith about the gravity of the situation and how important it is not to betray and how important it is to fulfil your covenant, so I'm sure in your mind, you're thinking about 'how do I break the covenant?' so now we'll speak about how one can break his covenant. There are two ways of breaking the covenant. [31:31]; by speech firstly; any statement which comes out that says that you're giving a person a covenant; that is understood to be a covenant – that becomes a covenant. For example, if you say 'welcome, come here, good morning, good day' all these type of statements, 'you're in safe hands here'; all these statements they indicate – or the other person will understand it to mean – that you are secure with this person; you are in safety with this person. And the one who is kicked out of their country, who is looking for asylum; one who is seeking political asylum for whatever reason; they're migrants, immigrants here – that's a more clear statement of asking and seeking for security … [33:24] The second type of this is the contract which is customary; how the people of that area, how they understand the covenant to be. To say, for example, getting the visa; an example of customary covenant is the visa. For example, the person got it from official channels and it says that you've got a visa to enter this country; there's no need for them to say it verbally – by getting the visa that's enough to say you've got *akuul amana* [i.e. a contract] between you and this country. Similarly, when a Muslim is working for a non-Muslim in his company, working for him, that means he's got a covenant of security with between the two parties. In the customary [covenant] we don't go to every person and we say to him: 'you are safe from me and I am safe from you; I'm not going to betray you; you aren't going to be betrayed me, whatever'; you don't say it this way but by working for him, by that reason, by that job, he is secure from you and you are secure from him and he's not allowed to betray you. It's customary that while you're working him and he's employing you, then both parties are happy or pleased or are happy with the situation that you are working for him and consequently that's a form of contract between you; a customary contract. [36:15] Similarly a person who is a student at university, you don't say to the university: 'I'm going to take a covenant of security with you; I'm not going to kill anyone' – people will be shocked if you said that. But it is customary that a person who is a student is not a fighter; the deal in a society where you're studying and you're in the university is that you don't have to take an akuul al-amana from them; rather, by you being there; the whole foundation of you being a student means that you're not a fighter; so by being in that situation you have taken a contract of studying with them means that you have a contract with them and you can't betray that."

Original link: http://islambase.co.uk/index.php?option=com_content&task=view&id=577&Itemid=181

The Centre for Social Cohesion

The Centre for Social Cohesion is a non-partisan think-tank that was set up by Civitas in 2007 to examine issues related to community cohesion in Britain. Headquartered in London, it was founded to promote new thinking that can help bring Britain's ethnic and religious communities closer together while strengthening British traditions of openness, tolerance and democracy.